Running Rebel and Mad Dog: A Memoir
Copyright ©2023 by Isobella Jade
First paperback edition, published in 2023 by HMS Books
Identifiers: ISBN 9798987562253 (print)
ISBN 9798987562246 (eBook)

The author has tried to re-create events and conversation based on their own memories and those of others. In some instances, in order to maintain anonymity, certain names and characteristics have been changed.

Cover design by Jazmin Ruotolo

Running Rebel and Mad Dog

A Memoir of Heirlooms Left Behind

Isobella Jade

HMS Books

HMS BOOKS

THE WALK TO THE CAR

The sirens howled down this country road, the twirling glow of red lights, the fire trucks lining the street near the long unplowed driveway that led to the barn, the place my father called home.

I can still see the tracks from the hoses, as I steady myself on the icy snow and walk to my Dad's white car. A blizzard had just gone by and the snowbanks are taller than me. I don't want to see the barn in the distance. I don't want to look at the charred remains and imagine Dad being unidentifiable. The fire happened on Saturday morning and now it's Wednesday, but the air still smells of singed wood planks and charred metal beams as I stand here.

It stings my nose.

Each muscle in my body is tight and tender, each breath strains my chest. It's swollen from my gag reflexes clenching up each time I cry and think of the smoke and fire bearing down on my Dad. I'm stuck in a dream somewhere between my Dad's voice and the sheriff's on the phone.

The small house is a converted barn in the countryside of Phoenix, New York. It was weird to me at first, the red structure had the appearance of an old storage shed, but my Dad was sure that this barn-turned-house was just the quiet place he needed. Only now it's no longer his peaceful home with his coffee pot by the kitchen sink and the round folding table by the window piled with his library books.

In the distance, chunks of debris and cinders cover the front of his home, the surrounding snow has turned black, and its bony frame is burnt from being enflamed. The rib cage of the barn is the only part intact. Holding up the barn are three red burnt walls remarkably still standing. There's a rectangle shape that was once the doorway, an opening where the kitchen window used to be, a grid of singed wood planks that made up the bathroom, and a big opening on the side of the structure. There are two windows on one wall, with huge smears of black smoke above them, stains where the smoke streamed out when the windows were blasted open by the explosion, and heat of the fire escaped. There's a huge gash on the roof as if the hand of God went in and ripped out the barn's heart.

I missed the first calls early in the morning on February 26th. The phone rang and rang, and I let it ring again. I'm 28, a newlywed, and sleeping in until noon on Saturday is typical, but this morning the phone was incessant. I finally answered.

The sheriff's voice had been gentle asking me if I was my Dad's daughter, "I hate to do this over the phone. There was a fire this morning, and we've located one victim in a hallway...There's one white car in the driveway registered in your Dad's name."

I shot out of bed.

My breath seeped deep inside of me. I replied that I was his daughter and said I would be back in a minute. I had hunched to the floor before the sheriff could continue. I was thinking about the last time I had spoken to my Dad. I held my breath, eyes shut, tears beginning, his face flashed through my mind: his wizard eyebrows, his jack-o-lantern smile, him hugging me goodbye at the train station, the smell of cigarettes and coffee. Had he been asleep when the fire broke out? Did he have time to run? What did he look like now? Why did this happen?

"Is he still there?" I asked softly.

"Yes, he is." the sheriff said. My father would not be moved from the hallway until the investigation was complete, he was still just lying there alone with the scorched remains of his home.

I wanted to run to him, unearth his body from the heavy scraps of wood and metal, shove the soot off him. But the sheriff said there was no need to hurry, they still needed to legally identify him, and he suggested I wait until after the autopsy. I want to be there, beside him, but I stay unmoved imagining what my father's face must look like.

My free-spirited self and the lightheartedness I walked with yesterday fled and became stiff as a board.

I had been working as a body part model going to castings and using my legs, hands and feet for photo-shoots. I recently booked a job for a nail polish editorial in a magazine, my hands holding the nail file gracefully, the color popping on my toes, among a lively landscape of beauty and perfection in a high-rise studio. Those years of building my portfolio and writing about these experiences, what I woke for each day, suddenly feels selfish, too unstable, a waste of time.

There had been words left unsaid.

Dad would leave me extra-long voicemails about his day and I hardly listened to them, I was too busy on to the next casting, a hopeful opportunity, or moving on from a recent rejection. I didn't leave much time for chit-chat. I should have really listened. I should have cared more. I want to talk to him, I want to say goodbye to my Dad. I hold the phone to my ear as my face scrunches up and I wipe my tears aside to speak with the sheriff some more.

"Is there a two-pocket flannel shirt?" I asked. "My Dad always wore one."

"It's not like that," the sheriff calmly told me. I wondered if maybe he slept shirtless. Then it struck me that the shirt must have burned away.

I imagine my Dad lying face down, his skin charred, slowly realizing the extremity of the explosion and fire and that my father was a part of the ash.

I was jerked from my thought when the sheriff asked, "Did your Dad wear any jewelry?"

"Like a ring?" I asked curiously. He had worn a maze-engraved ring as far back as I could remember.

"He has two silver rings. One has an engraving on it, like a maze; and one is just a silver band."

"Yes. There are two rings, one with an engraving," the sheriff said.

I felt nauseous and unsteady as I walked over to my bed. I wanted to curl up like a child. Those were his rings. I had given them to him. The original maze ring he loved had been stolen during a rough patch, some years back. I had seen a ring similar to it, at a silver jewelry street stand in Manhattan's fashionable SoHo district, so I bought it and gave it to him the next time I visited. I knew that this could only be my Dad, although legally the fingerprint would seal that it was him. Somehow the way that his body had fallen in the hallway must have allowed his hands to be spared enough from the fire. I had mentioned with some discomfort, not wanting to bring up Dad's DWIs to the sheriff right then, but that his fingerprints on file might help to compare Dad's postmortem fingerprints.

The sharp chill in the air chisels at my heart, my bare hands in my coat pockets, the wind in my face, unsure of what I will find in Dad's car. I imagine the quick moments: the tenth of a second before he lost his breath. Ice falling off the roof and cracking the propane line, gas leaking inside the barn, trickling to the baseboard heater. The explosion that blasted apart the early morning. The firemen struggling to get down the long unplowed driveway, dragging hoses through two feet of snow, rushing inside to put out the flames consuming the barn, blackening it from the inside out. Hearts racing, feet fast, arms swinging axes through scorched wood and throwing chunks of metal aside while they searched for him. A dark tent of smoke filling the sky above the barn.

Now my boots crunching over the snow are the only sound. He had to wait a few days, but I'm here. Just hold on, Dad. I'm coming. You're not alone, I had wanted to tell him. I yearned to let my Dad know I'd be here, after the investigation, after the medical examiner was finished with the autopsy, after the cremation was done, after he was secured in his urn. I'd be here. I'm bringing him back home with me to Manhattan today in the wooden urn I ordered the day after he died while still shaking in disbelief that it was happening.

Breathing in this smell of ash, my chest sinks into the core of me. He had only lived here into the fall and winter. And a few months ago, I had been here, a day before Thanksgiving visiting him. My husband and

I flew in from Manhattan, and after visiting with my Mom for a little while, we went to see my Dad at his new home.

He had moved around a lot over the past fifteen years. When I saw him a couple of times a year, we normally met at the Amtrak terminal in Syracuse or the library—anywhere but the place he was living at the moment. But there was assurance and relief in my father's voice, excitement for the fresh beginning here as he invited us into his home.

Whenever we talked on the phone, he entertained me with stories of his days—the stray cat he regularly fed through the fall, and the writing he intended to do among the peace and quiet. He had finally expressed a sense of calm in his "country life." This rural and farm area, where nearby the Seneca, Oneida and Oswego Rivers met, and the Three Rivers connected with the Erie Canal. Dad's home was right off Route 481 which led to Lake Ontario.

He wasn't living with a handful of lunatics, he said. I felt he was safe at the converted barn. I carried that thought in my mind while I rambled through New York City streets to a modeling booking, a photoshoot or casting, or writing in my journal, while I sat on a bench in Battery Park with the leaves changing color around me.

I could focus on other things.

My husband and I met him at the Nice N Easy gas station. We followed him down the country road, bumping and bouncing along the long driveway of dirt and leaves, heading down a gradual decline toward a red barn, and parked our cars side-by-side. We stepped out to give each other a hug. The damp cigarette smell on his coat was the same scent he always carried. He looked good. His glasses held their shape, his head was warm in his hat, he was freshly shaven, and his eyes were wide with glee. His teeth were crooked and coffee-stained and one looked a little loose, his eyebrows sprouting out wildly as always, rose up and down but with his big smile.

I took in my surroundings, this new place Dad called home. I saw a bowl of cat food outside. Instead of a huge barn double door, the front of the structure had been converted into a homey entryway. I smiled, and put my hand on his shoulder, as Dad fumbled with his keys and opened the door into a big living area and a kitchen to my right. Two large windows brought in light through the thin red curtains, making the brown-carpeted floor look more like amber.

Two plastic green lawn chairs represented the living room. Near them were a couple of metal filing boxes used as a coffee table. A small round folding table with a few library books on top sat by the window. There were a few other plastic chairs against the wall, but not much else to look at in the large room.

Dad took off his coat with a deep sigh. I knew he was working hard to survive and pay his rent and bills. He was almost sixty-three, and I wanted him to be able to enjoy the peace he craved. I made a mental note to buy him a couch and a writing desk. As he hung his coat on the back of one of the plastic chairs in the living room, I saw his signature flannel with pens bursting from the pockets. He had so much pep in his step as he gave us the grand tour. He said he'd be back in a flash and went out to smoke a cigarette. I leafed through the old Carl Sagan book *Cosmos* that he'd checked out from the library, awed by the photographs of bursts of color in outer space.

Then he told us stories about his life. It was as though, for the first time, he was settled enough to look back and reflect. I stared at his face, as if he was an old professor slouching in the chair, giving us philosophies on near misses, roads of regret and the willingness to accept what's been.

He grabbed a notebook, ripped out a few pages of his writings and thoughts on life, and handed them to me. I couldn't wait to read them. Sitting in the warmth of his home our conversation face to face was stretched out. We weren't rushed by a quick chat at the train station before the train arrived—that day at his home there was time.

Dad dashed back and forth to the kitchen, to us, back to the kitchen, offering us more coffee from his old pot and a pack of peanut-butter crackers. I held off going to the bathroom, not wanting to miss a word. By the time I stood up, I had forgotten we were sitting on old lawn chairs.

In between our conversation and crackers, I was imaging his life. It was quiet here, the sunlight came through the windows and he was making a better life in this place. He was doing okay, I told myself. I hugged him goodbye tightly and his cigarette smell stayed with me up the long driveway to the main road. He had finally seemed untroubled, with a lot to look forward to.

It didn't last long.

The red barn is no more. I swallow the freezing air, still filled with smut and burnt debris. Apart of me wishes he had never moved here, that he had five roommates and hadn't told me about the extra money he may need for the deposit for the place, I wish I had missed that phone call.

I knew the duties of putting Dad to rest and taking care of the details, were mine. It wasn't because I was the oldest daughter, it wasn't because I had done this type of thing before. I felt I was closest to my father; I had been the one who hung around the longest in his life. I knew I had to do this for him and didn't want his body to wait too long when I booked my flight to Syracuse.

Without a will, I had kind of winged it. I wrote the obituary in a rush; I had called a couple of Dad's family members who I hardly knew to confirm how many nieces and nephews he had and the correct spelling of the names of his four sisters and brother. Still there would be factual mistakes and gaps in my words that summed up his life. I confided in my younger sister to do the editing through back-and-forth emails, and we figured out how to word that there wouldn't be a funeral.

I would pick up copies of the newspaper with the published obituary and his urn both today.

When it came to a driver, instead of my husband I wanted my mom. She would be my driver since I'm the oldest person in America without my driver's license. She said on the phone we will spend the day doing anything I want to do.

My Mom is waiting in her car behind me, it has been many years since she has spoken to my dad, but she is here, driving me today so I can honor him. I met her in front of the Syracuse airport terminal, and we drove directly to my father's home.

Not getting to say goodbye was all I wanted to talk about. I thought there would be more time, I said. She gave me hugs, hand squeezes, understanding soft eyes, the space to cry into and as many tissues as I wanted. If she was thinking about their time together, the day they met, or what went wrong in their marriage, she didn't bring it up as we drove on the snowy roads. When we arrived, I told her I would be quick, but I knew I could take as long as I needed.

I don't try to walk down to the barn to get a closer look or dig around in the piles of debris. There's nothing left to claim.

I duck my head down into my coat against the wind as I walk to my father's car. I don't feel warm enough in the two-pocket flannel shirt I've worn in his honor.

Through the window I can see the car is littered in trash. All the papers and folders add up to an office that's never been organized. I remember the sheriff telling me on the phone there was food in the car, as if my Dad had just gone grocery shopping. I reach for the handle of the passenger side door. The doors are unlocked, my Dad didn't feel the need to lock his car out here.

I slip into the passenger seat, its shelter protecting me from the cold. I push a few coffee cups and newspapers aside and just sit there for a minute, among all that's left of his world. The smell of Newport cigarettes and old attic that used to cling to my Dad now consumes me. This car was his comfort zone, he sat here every day, a place full of him. I've never been in it before now, and I wish he was here with me, moving aside his supplies, sitting in the driver's seat, talking to me face to face. I've cried so hard since Saturday that my body feels dry and curled up like an old orange peel. My eyes squint from exhaustion.

I scavenge through scraps of paper, half-broken pens, a stack of coffee-stained folders and envelopes, and many other random bits that look like they belong in the trash. But these are the artifacts of my Dad's life. Anything with his handwriting on it catches my eye, and is put in a pile of remembrance.

Opening the glove box, I see the pocketbook that holds the car registration and insurance documents. Looking at these papers, I could almost hear him telling me about the used snow tires he had just bought. I knew how much having this car meant to him, since he didn't always have a vehicle of his own.

In one of the cup holders is his thermos. The liquid is completely frozen inside, still I smell the strong scent of dark coffee when I sniff the rim. After rehab and finally recovering from his alcoholism, he always drank a lot of coffee. The smell of the thermos reminds me of our chats at the train station where we'd meet and talk at a table with our coffee cups between us. He'd talk fast, peppy from the caffeine while we caught up face to face.

In the other cup holder, I find a pocket knife, a couple of keys and nail clippers, all held together by a weak key ring. He gave me a pocket knife like this one when I was in middle school. My parents had already been separated for a few years, and the house my Dad was living in at the time was the same house we had all lived in together. He was working for the local newspaper selling subscriptions but wasn't pulling in enough money. He said the house was all he had. Over the phone my Dad told me that he wanted to die, and he hoped that he could wait until I graduated high school.

Behind the driver's seat there are more strewn newspapers and receipts. A cardboard box full of home-improvement fliers sits next to another one filled with jarred foods, cans of tuna, baked beans, peas and corn, peanut butter and jelly, apple sauce, a bag of frozen oranges—all from a food bank. Among these pantry items are many empty packs of Newports.

Digging under the food box, I find his old, stained Giant's football cap. I crack a little smile thinking about him wearing it. The smashed hat is damp and musty and has probably been buried in here since the summer.

My fingers touch the brim where he tried to hand sew it back together. I take a deep breath remembering how it looks a lot like the ragged one he wore to a couple of my high school track meets.

It doesn't seem real that I'm now the owner of these old things until I see the sports jacket. It's hanging neatly on the coat hanger of the backseat door, with his extra two-pocket dress shirts—he was always the ready salesman. I smile at his enthusiasm for knocking on doors, handing out fliers, and making calls from gas stations and coffee shops to get a lead. He liked to dress for the part. He knew the clean, straight lines of the collar and brass buttons on the sports jacket were part of the pitch.

How can I be touching my father's sports jacket without his arms in the sleeves giving me a hug? When I press my face into the collar, the well-worn fabric feels slightly scratchy and I get a whiff of cigarettes. I hold up the jacket a little and rest my face against the shoulder. When I go through the pockets I pull out some used tissues and eight sugar packets. In an inner pocket there's a pen with his name on it. I stare at it for a second more: "Home remodelers and alarms, small business solutions, personal counseling"—his dreams, printed around the pen. I put the tissues, sugar packets and the pen back in his pockets for safekeeping, just as he had left them.

Weeding through more papers in the backseat, I search for anything of worth—anything he might have worn recently or used day-to-day. I look for handwritten notes with some of his thoughts or appointments he might have scheduled, details that might give me a closer glimpse into his life. I find his handwriting all over a flier attached to a wooden clipboard that he must have used often. His business card is clipped to it for his sales work with construction companies.

Hidden among more trash on the backseats, I'm surprised to find a bright orange pocket-sized New Testament with Psalms and Proverbs. I open it up and see that he wrote his name and phone number on the inside cover.

Growing up, the name Jesus was something I heard when the car stalled or when Dad's leg had to be wrapped in a big white brace because of gout pains. Recently, though, he had begun to go to church up here, and had told me that he enjoyed socializing during the coffee hour after the service. He had even asked the pastor how he could be of help in the food pantry or in any other way. I'm sure he liked the free coffee and the opportunity to talk about comprehending the mysteries of the universe—the purpose of all things.

My faith is full of doubt—I don't believe it was his time, or that he's in a better place now. I don't know if my soul will one day be stronger. This converted barn and open land around his home was supposed to be his second chance. I want to wilt into the backseat of his car. He was here less than a week ago, drinking from his thermos and listening to an oldies song on the radio. I slowly place the small bible in my pile of heirlooms.

Taking one last look, underneath some trash on the floor of the backseat, I see a very old, brown, boondoggle leather wallet. I almost missed it. I'm stunned, and my astonishment is due to its age, and that it's the most special treasure I've found. I made it for him the summer before I turned nine years old, during a free arts and craft class. This was the last year we spent as a family. The summer when I was unsure, but he encouraged me to run all the way around the dirt track myself. He believed in me, before I believed in myself.

Made of leather and threaded with plastic string that is coming un-done, it's held together with rubber bands, but he treasured it. He still had it after all these years. He opened it a million times. I remember how he'd pull it out to hand me a few bucks when he was doing okay.

I thought about a voicemail Dad had left me at Christmas time, after my younger sister had visited him at the barn. It was first time they had seen each other in years, and they had made amends. I imagine our dad opening his worn-out wallet to show her that he still had a photo of her inside, even if it was tattered from the years. Seeing how beat-up his wallet was, she had given him a gift card to buy a new one.

So, I have found his old one, the only wallet I can imagine him using. He must have thrown it in the backseat of his car after he bought a new one. It feels like I'm holding his hand as I turn the aged leather around. If my sister hadn't visited him, it would have gone with the flames. I look inside. It's full of coupons and old receipts. There's bent photos, wrinkled with time, of my sister and me sitting together on our couch, being silly little girls. Our little scribbled handwriting is on the back of another photo. Our senior pictures from high school are there too. He carried us with him wherever he went. I wrap the rubber band back around the wallet.

Then my own handwriting catches my eye. There are cards and letters I'd sent my father over the years that he saved in folders; one has my signature rose drawing on it. The Starbucks card I sent him was clearly used and tossed.

The trunk is jam-packed. I don't have time to go through it fully, but I see there is even a toilet in there for some reason! I roll my eyes at the absurdity and think about Dad's peculiar ways of finding use or wanting to fix old and broken things. I am only in town for a day. My flight will leave in a few hours. I throw what I can into trash bags as the wind goes wild. I'm tensed up and torn inside. When I exhale, my warm breath hits the cold air, creating the effect of smoke around me. My pile looks small. I put the bundle in my duffle bag. These items, unintended by my father to become his keepsakes, these leftovers of his life, suddenly hold a luster and become more valuable in their deeper meaning.

The wind pushes me into my Mom's car, and she gives me a warm smile and rubs my hands. I can hardly look into her sad eyes. Neither of us know what to say as she drives out of the driveway and onto the country road.

"Can we turn left first?" I ask. I want to see my Dad's place one more time. She drives slowly, and I stare at the tracks made by fire trucks and hoses in the snow, and the remains of the red structure. I should've called more and not rolled my eyes at his long voicemails, because now I'm trying to search for what he'd tell me, and I just can't hear it. I start to unravel. This is it. My Mom pulls to a side road, and we sit here, where my Dad lived, for a moment more. I cover my face, and the tears come fast.

He had left me a voicemail the day before he died. The unknown of tomorrow hadn't happened yet, he ended the message saying, "...remember absence makes heart grow fonder, familiarity breeds contempt and... out of sight out of mind. Anyways we got ourselves another blizzard. And...we'll talk soon, love you honey, bye bye." I've played it over and over since the sheriff's call.

It's around 2 p.m. when I get to the funeral home, housed in a big brick building that looks like a mansion. Strange phases of sleepiness and hyperactivity have been battling inside me over the past few days. I can't even think about sleep until his urn is with me. I want to know my

Dad has somewhere to rest. The sidewalk is freshly shoveled in front of the snow banks.

I walk soft-footed up the pathway, hugging myself against the wind. I delicately ring the doorbell and my stomach is filled with huge knots. A man with a shaved head wearing a suit and a friendly smile opens the door grandly. I can tell from his nod that he's been expecting me when I tell him, "I'm here to pick up my Dad's urn."

It's a quiet afternoon here. I pass a big room with chairs set up in rows. The carpets are a blue-gray, the walls are cream, the antiques are situated with care, and all the furniture is refined and delicate. We pass a fireplace and I inhale deeply. I'm skittish and antsy. "It's so pretty in here—like a museum," I tell the funeral director. He smiles and directs me to his office, where he welcomes me to sit down in a comfortable Victorian-style chair.

I stand for a moment. In front of me is a wooden urn, a little bigger than a shoe box, with a mountainous landscape and valley of pine trees carved into the wood.

My Dad. In the urn. Right on the desk. Right in my face.

I didn't expect to see it resting there, waiting for me. Staring back at me.

"Here's the urn," the funeral director says calmly.

I stare at the carving, the clouds, and the pine trees. I take in every detail; the round corners, the layered ridges of wood at the top. I'm sure my Dad would've approved. In the quietness, I'm overwhelmed with such a longing to see him again, to hear his voice. I'm on the verge of tears. My instinct is to pick it up. It's heavy, the weight of a bowling ball. I sit down holding it, hugging it in my lap.

I thank the funeral director for all his help preparing everything so quickly. He gives me the plastic baggie from the medical examiner's office. My shoulders sink. Inside are my Dad's two rings; the plain silver band and the silver ring with the maze-like engraving. Seeing them tarnished with black soot, all dirty inside the creases of the intricate design, makes my heart raw.

The urn starts to feel heavier in my lap. I'm holding all that's left of my Dad. Signing some final paperwork, I feel my eyes burning, but take a deep breath to hold in my cries. Outside, the sun is shining on this cold day, the icy patches of snow glistening. I balance the urn straight across my arms like I'm carrying a birthday cake to mom's car, and somehow relief finds me. I'm almost done here.

I pull the urn out of a canvas tote bag.

"What's inside?" asks the Transportation Security Administration officer at the airport. Light-headed, I almost smile when I tell him it's my Dad. I'm so nervous that the TSA officer would ask to remove the screws at the bottom of the urn to see what was inside. I was uneasy holding it. I place it on the security conveyor belt and there it goes through the security X-ray tunnel, along with my carry-on duffle bag with the heirlooms.

The plane is small, and the urn just fits under the seat in front of me. Once we are in the air, I place it on the empty seat next to me. I use my canvas bag as a cover over the urn and I lay down, resting on it, my little pillow, all the way home to New York City.

The taxi driver who picks me up at the airport offers to help carry the bag with the urn and put it in the trunk, but I hold onto it. The blue lights of the Brooklyn Bridge are coming closer. "Isn't it beautiful, Dad? This is what I've seen every day." I want to walk with him on these streets of Manhattan, and catch up on all his stories, the one about getting his tires rotated and how he didn't need to spend a hundred dollars on new tires when he could get used ones for twenty. Or the time he plunged the toilet at a coffee shop just because it's common sense to do he said, "it didn't take a committee to figure it out, you only had to lift and pull." Then the zip in his voice about the free coffee he received. I used to tune out his chatter but now I want to hear it all.

When I enter my apartment, I keep the lights off for a few minutes. Out of the living room window the lights on the boats passing by make red and blue dots on the Hudson River. I carry my Dad's urn around the apartment, deciding where to put it. I love how the sun comes through the windows so brightly in the morning, big rays bouncing off the river and into the apartment, so I place the urn on the coffee table facing the windows. I don't want him to get too hot there—he never liked the heat—but I want him to see each new day start with the sun coming into the apartment. I place his pocket knife on top of his urn and his thermos beside it.

He never visited me here. He said he didn't like the hustle and bustle of the city, so I never invited him, and yet his remains are now in my living room. *This is where I live, Dad. This is your home now. You are safe with me.*

I crouch down and put my arms around the urn.

After this day, I'll be scared for a long while and have difficulty sleeping—paranoid that the stove isn't off, or that I forgot to unplug the iron, and that something will catch fire. Night after night, I'll lie in bed, unable to calm my mind, thinking about how the morning is unknown, and try to make peace with the fact that some people don't get a tomorrow.

That first morning though, the sun is melting the ice on the Hudson River. Its golden rays bathe the corner of my Dad's urn. I go through my bounty of keepsakes again: the sports jacket, the coffee thermos, the clipboard and his handwriting on the flyers, the old brown leather wallet, the small orange New Testament, the Giants cap, his rings, pocketknife, and old letters and cards. They carry with them his scent, his wit, his charming crooked smile. The tough times he'd been through and the way he had just missed the gateway for a quiet, calmer life—it's all held dear within the creases and crevices of these possessions. When I look at these objects, I see more than their shape and function, I see the years of his life unwind, the way he and I connected over our belief in new beginnings—the reasons I believed in him. I didn't know then that these heirlooms would spark my interest to uncover what I didn't know about my father, what held our relationship up, all it lacked, and what he left behind.

WHAT I DIDN'T KNOW

It has just passed five years since my father died, and I'm now over sixteen hundred miles away from Manhattan and even further from my hometown near Syracuse, New York. My kids grow faster than these weeds around me, Phoenix is starting pre-K and Vivian is toddling around. They are smashing water balloons on each other and running through the sprinkler in our backyard here in Texas. The humidity is no bother, nothing slows them down as they plow into this new southern life. They have already forgotten the city they were born in, the ice cream shop a block away, the diner we loved right below the high rise we lived in, where they gobbled up pancakes and sausages. Not long ago they were running to the slide at the playground by the East River in Manhattan, watching the sea lions at the zoo in Central Park and blissfully throwing pennies in the Bethesda fountain.

A year after my father died, I measured where to fit a small crib. I had written in my journal an entry directed to my father. *There's a little life in me. I've taken an immense amount of pregnancy tests and all positive, there is a pulling at my stomach and pinching below my belly button on mostly my right side, sometimes left. If you were alive and I could call you I'd tell you and share this with you.*

When someone asks why I named my son Phoenix, I first say the mystical bird, but then I follow with explaining its the name of the town my father lived in before he died. Naming my son in honor of the place my father died helped to soften the ache I was carrying when I became a mother. I could say the name and fill it with love, the name would hold my heart and be a comfort for my grief.

Then I became completely swaddled up with two kids a couple years apart. It kept me going to watch their lives begin, their busy-bodied lives aided the brokenness I felt inside. The duffle bag was kept out of toddler reach. I could stroll on and carry this slice to my chest while sipping coffee and maneuvering the double stroller one-handed, whizzing across 79th street, past Lexington, Park and Madison Avenue, a quick left on Fifth Avenue and onward to the Central Park zoo.

In their every smile, while taking photos of the dinosaur bones at the science museum, doused in every water pad at every playground, my handbag packed with snacks and steering them forward, my grief was kept at bay, silent in my chest, while encouraging those first little steps of life.

Then everything changed.

I was reluctant to move to Texas, to leave behind New York state and where I had grown up, I didn't agree for the long term, but for the sake of family togetherness, and my marriage, I surrendered and let it go. I didn't know I would be going through a divorce in a few years, I would be alone, in a place I never intended to be, sharing time with my kids, and I didn't know yet my father's death wouldn't be the greatest grief of my life.

Instead, I packed up our belongings, some to be shipped by moving truck, other items in suitcases, and my father's urn was once again my carry-on item, under the seat in front of me, on a plane headed to Houston.

In the still uncertainty of my new surroundings, I sat back on a lawn chair and my shoulders dropped, the mass of blue sky, the freshly cut grass, the size of the yard, the shed and sunshine making me dehydrated, it didn't feel like mine. The unfamiliar, forty minutes outside of Houston, and the smell of the blood from the pig farm across my cookie-cutter neighborhood. I could die in the isolation of open space.

In my attempt and fail at a garden, the damn dying tomato plant—a longing for my roots pops up, a gust of crisp wind, a thirst to keep where I come from with me, and that's when I thought about opening the duffel bag that holds my father's possessions.

I realize that if I don't explore the deeper meaning in my father's heirlooms that sit buried in this bag, I will leave my father behind. The barn has been knocked down by now, the plot of land, probably has grass shooting up from the gash in the ground by now.

In the silence of my life shifting to a new zip code, I have a sudden urge to look back and uncover what is uncertain, I need to know that my father lived a good life, I need to know something good to tell my children about his life.

I didn't think much about claiming my father's health records and I took my time to retrieve the document, letting years go by and figuring it would consist of basic health stats, but when I finally went after my father's health history the records revealed more than I expected. I never imagined the trove spanning twenty years and over one hundred pages of his whereabouts, his mental health, depression, and so much of what he never told me laid on these pages.

While I scrolled the CD, I knew I would have to print it. I would carry sections with me, I'd read them in the car line while picking my son up from school, at soccer practice, or while my daughter played with slime. The pages were coffee stained, stuck together, beat up and torn from being tossed in my handbag. My little girl would do somersaults until the sun went down and my son would score goals and then we'd order Chic-Fil-A and the warm bag of food would lay on top of these pages, stuffed between daily life, and I would learn a little more about what I didn't know.

WALLET

The Texas grass tickles the ankles of my children, Phoenix and Vivian ask me to time them, and to say, "Ready, Set, Go!" I pretend I have a stopwatch, and while they race each other across the yard, I think back to all the running I did with my father, the summer I was eight—the summer I made him a wallet, and how special it was to find it in his car after he died.

Dad drags his shoe across the dirt, in a big, long scrape, perfecting our starting line as he does each time we come to the dirt track. I stretch my legs, mosquito bites all over, and I feel the small bumps and some new scabs on my knees as I look across the widespread vacant field. Dad and I are the only ones at the track.

The sun is high and makes his forehead look shiny; there's no shade here. My shoes crunch on the track while I stretch. The dirt track at the field behind the Zogg building has been left to waste away, it's a blend of cinder, crushed gravel and stones. Any track lanes are now eroded. The path dips low in some places, with bruises as deep as potholes.

The windows on the Zogg building are grainy and shadowed, so that it looks more like a haunted mansion than the very first high school in the village of Liverpool, New York. It's named for Alfred Valentine Zogg, who had been a principal here. The school closed a year before I was born and is now an administrative building that sits as a prestigious landmark in our town, but it's a little spooky with the run-down open field and dirt track in the back. Dad and I just call it Zogg.

We are ten minutes outside of the city of Syracuse. It snows up the steps to the door in the winter, but in the summer Dad says, "Hell couldn't be hotter."

At the track he lets out a sigh and runs his hands through his poufy hair. He takes his glasses off for a moment and with the sleeves of his shirt he wipes the sweat off his forehead. We aren't big on sunscreen and I get real tan in the summer like Mom. A sunshine glow is always on her face, but Dad has lighter skin and freckles on his arms, and he doesn't like being out in the heat for too long. I worry that at any moment he will say, "That's it. That's enough of this heat."

There were only a few more weeks until school started, and a few more weeks of running. The sun would go down earlier, he'd be busier with his work as the landlord at the white house behind ours on 6th Street, fixing anything that ever needs fixing, or listening to his sales messages on the answering machine. The heat of the August sun would be gone, along with his voice calling me down the last stretch of track.

"You'll be really close to double digits soon," Dad says with a kooky smile. I'd be nine in early September. Maybe it was because I was growing older, wasn't as whiny and could run further, that Dad had begun spending more time with me. Maybe, though, it was because of the hand-stitched brown leather wallet I'd given him only a month before.

That summer, I had taken several free arts-and-crafts classes at my elementary school. In one, I had learned how to make lanyard bracelets. In another, I learned how to use that same plastic string to sew through leather. The choices were a coin purse or a wallet and I had chosen to make a wallet for Dad. I wanted the wallet to be perfect. I didn't mind being the last one finished. My hands laced the plastic thread through the pre-holed brown leather so carefully. Worried the string of the boondoggle wasn't pulled together tight enough on the edges, I was looping and tightening it with each pull around the edges, binding it neatly. It was sturdy when I was done, and I opened and closed it a few times to test its durability before going home.

I whacked open our screen door, bringing into our house some of the summer air, and presented it to Dad, bursting with pride.

"I made this for you," I said.

His eyebrow arched above his big round glasses as he examined it. His fingers went across the smooth leather and strummed down each shiny bump of the plastic string that went around the wallet's edges. Even though it didn't shut fully on its own, and he used a rubber band around it to keep it closed, he had it with him from that day on. It made a bulgy square in his back pocket and was full of coupons and receipts from Nichols, our little village grocery store. He quickly filled the wallet with photos of my younger sister and me, lined up side-by-side so they could be flipped through, to see grainy photos of togetherness. When I didn't know where Dad was, or if he was too tired to get up in the morning with us, which was most days, I knew his wallet was with him, which meant part of me was with him too.

That summer, Dad began timing me at the dirt track. If I could create a functioning wallet, he said, then I could run all the way around the track. The dirt track was new ground for me to suddenly to build roots into. Other summers Dad ran with me, starting me off the first hundred meters of the 400-meter track, letting me run ahead of him. Running as fast as we could was sort of a silly game then. He would fade behind me perhaps purposely, adjusting his glasses slipping off his face. When going all the way around the track seemed too big of a distance for me, we ended the race before the curve going for the 200-meter mark.

Now we take running seriously. The purpose of going to the track is to improve each time. This summer has ended up to be the best time I've ever spent with Dad, we had this carved out time to bond, just him and I.

Although an hour before, I had almost lost hope we'd make it to the track today. As Dad slept on the couch, I purposely let out a deep sigh in hopes he'd hear me and open his eyes. Mom had asked him if he was too tired to watch me while she took my sister school shopping. At first, I jumped up at the sound of buying something new, asking if I could go, but then changed my mind.

Dad said he would take me to the track, and I wanted to go with him. I didn't care about a new outfit so much. I didn't want to think about this summer ending right now. I wanted to keep it going. I smiled at her to let her know I'd be okay, as he mumbled about a headache. He went back to sleep after she left. The big white fans hummed throughout the house with the putter of Dad's snores. He was curled up on the couch using the arm rest as a pillow, his hair an overgrown mess. I put on my sneakers with pink hearts, double knotting them. It seemed like he was going to sleep all day. As I peered over the filing cabinet in the dining room, there was Dad's wallet. I unwrapped the rubber band from around it, perfect brown string holding it together at the seams.

Inside, I admire the pictures of our family, all smiles and in one I'm holding my favorite pink bear. I look at Dad's driver's license picture and count all the receipts. When the couch creaked, I wrapped the rubber band around the wallet and put it back to its place on top of the filing cabinet, safe and sound.

I stepped back when Dad's eyes opened. Yawning into a stand, his arms stretched up to the mint-green ceiling, he put on his glasses and then caught his balance. I stepped back, giving him room to wake up. I followed him, being extra "careful and quiet, and almost invisible" while he said those words on the way to the bathroom as advice to me.

He rubbed his legs, complained about some pain from gout in his knee and the need to refill his medication. I stood in the bathroom doorway, eager to go to the track as he coughed heavily between his toothpaste spits, leaning over the sink his body hunched, hacking as though a wild beast, he might have thrown up.

I retied my shoes tighter.

Back in the kitchen, he opened the refrigerator. A handmade Mother's Day card we all made for Mom last spring was still stuck on the door with a magnet. I had drawn a blue flower on it, my careful handwriting spelling out how much we loved her. My sister drew a stick figure of our Mom. Dad had written inside the card, "You are the glue." I had followed with writing, "that holds us together." Dad had signed the card for us, and added "with love, Curt."

I've never heard my parents reminisce or share memories of being together before they had children. I've seen a few photographs of them together though, one is at their wedding. They are standing behind the wedding cake, Mom is wearing a pink flowered dress that she made herself. She has large eyeglasses, long brunette hair, and a band of daisies around her head. Her smile is sincere, on this happiest day of her life, she's beautiful. Dad is in a white tux, with curly-q untamed red hair and a long beard. His eyes are half open, as though he just got off a fast ride at a carnival, with a huge smile and his head tilts slightly downward as though it's an unsteady attempt to create a perfect cake-cutting moment of them together.

In another photo while in college, they look so young. They are sitting in the sand at a beach and my father is sleeping on my mother's legs, and she is smiling with her arm around him.

In my baby book, there's a photograph of my parents standing close, with the back steps of the green house behind them. Dad has an arm around mom, she smiles warmly while holding me, a newborn. Dad has a small glass of beer in his hand, his glasses are off, his hair still curly, eyes beaming. It's one of the only photos of me and both of my parents.

They don't seem as close now, they aren't together too often, and we don't have big outings all together.

There's a photograph in the family album with my sister smiling at the neighborhood public pool, with the same facial expression our Dad has, one eyebrow up, one down. Once in a while she listens to Dad singing on the porch with me, and when he sings "Poor Little Fool," by Ricky Nelson, he's not calling us fools, I remind her that he's just singing about himself. I could sense in the way she stood by me and not him, that his smoky smell and expressive eyes could be a little intense for her.

Although in another photo my sister's up on Dad's shoulders, holding his forehead with her small hands, full happiness on her face. In another, we are on his back while he crawls on the ground as a warthog would, snorting around. It's clear we had togetherness, we played and laughed, even if it was brief.

She will unfortunately never really know him, and he'd be more of a stranger to her than a father.

I had been around Dad's stumbling around longer, and to me it became the usual. Dad's kooky smile was funny to me, not as scary as it seemed to my little sister. Perhaps if I hadn't been born first my impression would be different.

As children it's hard to imagine that our parents had lives of their own before us. They had less responsibility, and flourished with their independence, when they had years and a whole world ahead of them, that changed with our existence.

The deeper complexities of our parents can get muffled behind the day-to-day of fulfilling our needs. We only see a part of them, and we do not know what's at their core, beyond how they carry themselves while with us.

But once in a while, we see a glimpse of that person they had been, with a certain tilt of a hat, or maybe from earrings brought out from a small gift box that sparkle and light up their face in an unfamiliar way, or when a song comes on that makes them stand up and dance so carefree, singing the lyrics so passionately. An old photograph might reveal not just a different hairstyle, but their earlier interests, what inspired them—rich clues to the life experiences that makes us who we are.

I wonder what my son will think when he sees pictures of me modeling or traipsing around New York City. When my little girl asks for the lipstick I'm using, she doesn't know of the years I spent trying to make it in modeling, even though it would have been easier to just give up and trash my portfolio with all the no's. I think of the critical eyes of many magazine editors, photographers and art directors deciding if my skin tone was what they were looking for, or the stern faces of casting agents when they said, "Thanks for coming," and those slow months when I lived on dollar-menus and was unsure if my chance would ever come.

In my closet inside a storage box, I keep my portfolio of tear sheets from national magazines and brands from jobs I finally booked when I worked as a body part model. It took years to fill it. It's mostly of hands, legs and feet—besides the bookings when my ass was needed! I once went fully nude on the set of a fashion reality television series. When my modeling agent had asked, "interested in a nude?" it was no problem. I was the girl for it. I was comfortable flaunting what I had. I did a lot of body jobs, where I showed off my figure. I flung my towel off and strutted on the set. When the television host said to the full audience, "Now how can I get a body like that?" I turned and twirled a few times, graciously taking the compliment.

Those experiences in front of the camera seem forever ago. While preparing mac and cheese and unsticking goo from the cervices of furniture and strollers, I've grown comfortable with my mom-body and my increased jean size, but I haven't been in a bikini in years, and my belly after two kids is not something I flaunt.

I smile though at the thought of being pampered before a magazine photoshoot and how pretty my nails and skin looked then. Although further down in the box are other images in large envelopes and on CDs. These do not bring out my best side. They show my super platform high heels, my arms pushing together my small bare breasts, I am teasing the camera with mysterious eyes that said trashy more than alluring. I roll my eyes at my foolishness; these photos remind me of regrets in front of the camera. I might throw them out.

Will my children ever know that I didn't have a clean-cut path? I hope they see that although I didn't go as far as I wanted, I had somehow filled this portfolio as proof that I was someone who hung on and took chances.

When I think of these low points, I remember my Dad encouraging me, saying, "You *will* make it." It felt like if I did, then it would be a story we both shared. I realize how similar we were, despite how long it had been since we had real quality time together, like long ago when I was just a kid in my running sneakers.

Dad shut the fridge, deciding he'd go without an omelet. Midday omelets were his specialty, slopping together the eggs and cheese, often with an old onion turning brown, or a bruised tomato from Mom's garden, chopping on his creation, slurping up the falling pieces that usually spilled out of his mouth. Instead, he grabbed a handful of saltine crackers and handed me a stack; there's a cigarette behind his ear, a lighter in his pocket. Finally, he was ready to take me to the track.

Before we left he would check on his wallet on top of the filing cabinet but decide to leave it there for safekeeping. We only live two houses away from Zogg.

"It's easier to move around without it. We won't be gone too long." He had said before we left.

"I bet you'll be faster this time." His smile showed he had no doubt I would be.

I hear our dog, Heidi who is just a year older than me and sometimes looks like a black and brown wolf. Her nails clattered down the back stairs with us, she barked as we left, and followed us on her long chain to as far as she could, on our way to the track.

"Alright, are you ready?" Dad's loud voice bounces off the windows of the Zogg building behind us and sets us in motion.

I do my last stretch with arms to the sky. My shoes skittish and ready to move upon the small stones and dirt. I line up and join Dad so we're standing side-by-side. I'm a little thirsty already, but I know he will tell me we can get water right after this race, and give me a lecture about how long human beings can survive without water, so I stay quiet.

"Remember, like this," he says.

He bends his body down in race position, one arm forward and one arm back, one leg forward and one leg back. He's frozen in stride. I bend my body down and place my arms like his, as a real runner would. I stare down the first 100 meters.

"On your mark, dear," He's the announcer using his dignified Shakespearian accent.

I wait for his next call. He presses the buttons on his fancy sport watch recently purchased from a thrift store, and taps the timer ready.

"Set." He says in a deeper tone.

"Get your arms right," He reminds me.

I do.

Then in a deeper voice Dad says it all again quickly, "OnYourMark-SetGo!"

With the beep of his watch, I dart out with a huge stride into the first straight away, arms pumping fast, upper cutting the sky with my fists, small stones flipping beneath my feet. I pounded the air in front of me, elbows up, and stretching my stride to see how fast my legs can go during the first 100 meters. My legs are on fire.

"Go, Running Rebel, go," Dad yells after me.

I feel strong, my scuffed-up shoes with small hearts were fast. My arms swing back and forth, my engines working against time. I could hear him behind me, "Remember keep your arms high—your arms make your legs go faster..."

My arms chopping down each second, jabbing the air.

"Breath, breath—breathing makes you faster." Dad says with a bigger yell.

My heart slipped into the groove, my eyes looking ahead, determined to be faster this time. I'm not the girl who is too sensitive and timid when my name is called at school. This summer, on this track, I'm braver than I've ever been.

While I zoom down the first 100 meters, in the corner of my eye, across the street for a few seconds I can see the back of our house, the only mint-green one on 5th Street. I am breathing heavy, but could still hear Heidi, howling like a wolf across the street in our backyard, pacing the wire fence. She is barking and barking as I run further and further down the track.

Dad's voice has become faint as I run further away but I can hear him saying, "Keep going...keep going."

I focus on the curve of the track ahead, the long one I need to be ready for. If I weakened there, it would change my time. I want to be faster than I ever been—Dad believes I can be.

The chance to be faster this time sways through my ponytail, my heart and skinny legs are working for it. I feel taller on the track, my limbs long, breathing into the heat and dirt as I dash forward. I pass the long jump pit, our landing marks from the other day are still in the sand. Now, the first 100 meters are behind me and I veer as if nothing could stop me into the 200-meter-long bend.

My arms slicing the air down. Every step reminds me of another second passing on Dad's watch. I run the curves of the track hard. The harder I run them the faster I will be in the end. "The curves are where the winner is made." Make the curves count." Dad said when we practiced.

I try to widen my stride, thinking that I shouldn't have blasted out from the starting line so fast. I need to save some energy also for the other long straightaway, across the grassy field that seemed never-ending. I usually wanted to fall to the ground there, it was where the muscles behind my knees got tight, as if they were splitting apart.

I look over across the wide field. Dad is a smudge of white from his shirt and blue from his cut off denim shorts. I bet he's checking his stop watch, predicting my time down to the tenth of a second.

The distance hit me. I'm alone with the liberty of dirt and air. Within the solitude I feel more grown, listening to my breathing and my deep exhales, I'm arriving at full speed.

While I run, the uneven line of bangs across my forehead isn't as noticeable. The constant knotty snarl in the back of my hair is pulled up and hidden in the tie of my ponytail. My secondhand shorts are suddenly as good as new and keep me moving swiftly. My t-shirt with a few stains is proof I'm working with all my might. My overbite and the gap between my teeth are a blur as I rush by. My old running shoes kicking up smalls stones against my calves is a reminder that I'm going to make it and be faster this time.

"You don't have to be tall to be fast. If your legs are strong you can be just as fast," Dad would remind me during pep talks. He had told me about Muggsy Bogues, who at 5 ft. 3 inches, was the shortest basketball player ever in the NBA, but was able to keep up with the bigger, taller, all-stars like Reggie Miller and Scottie Pippin. He told me that Natalie Wood, the actress in his favorite film, *Rebel Without a Cause*, was only five feet tall. Part of the nickname Dad gave me, Running Rebel, comes from that movie, with James Dean as the rebel.

My legs thump on the track, and that feeling of quitting that always shows up around here is clawing at my ankles. The straight stretch that goes on forever is next. My heavy inhales and exhales fill my ears. My thighs feel as though jugs of milk are attached to them. Apart of me wants to just tell Dad I can't make it and fall to ground because being faster is impossible. He was way on the other side of the field. I push my legs forward. He was waiting to call me into the final curve of the track, if I ever got there.

I try to find a song in my head, a beat to run to, a rhythm to keep me going, an oldie song that Dad sings on the window-enclosed porch at the front of our hundred-year-old house.

Dad sang in three places: the basement, dining room, and out on the porch. Out there he would sit, a cloud of smoke around him, holding a newspaper and a pen in hand while singing with the radio.

On the porch the sun hit the side of his cheek and I could see an old red tint show up in his hair when he sang a song about the sunshine being gone, or another oldie about sitting on a dock watching the sun going down. He had been circling jobs he might consider applying for, but when I looked over his shoulder, I saw there were only circles around a few classified ads for junk on sale. "I could fix this bike, and sell it for double, maybe triple." he said, seriously considering it out loud.

It sounded like a good plan, he had fixed my bike chain plenty of times.

Standing there with him he reaches for the red and white can and took a deep gulp. I admire the red curvy pretty letters on the can and the capital B, then U, then D, of the strange long word that Dad has told me is a German word. There's a whole world out there, Dad likes to remind me. With the puffs of smoke around him, the bitter smell completes him.

His voice pepped up with a handsome wink when he sang with Ricky Nelson my favorite song about traveling the world. Dad sang every part of the song, the bum, bum, bums in the background too, not missing a melody change. His face so involved with the song, moving his expressions to match the mood of each line. It's like a musical geography class for me while he sang about traveling to different countries and the girls he knew in each country. He took off his glasses for a few beats just to give me one of his James Dean smirks. His drink had become a background slurp that blended into the faster pace rock and roll and doo-wop rhythm as he sang into another oldie song.

When the sun is gone, the melody changed and so did Dad's face. The lines on his forehead became deeper above his eyes. I liked how mysterious his profile looked in shadow while sitting by the window in the dining room near the speakers. The orange fire at the end of his cigarette glowed in the darkened room as he took a long drag. I only listened as Dad hummed and sang from somewhere deep inside of him, from a place he didn't share with me.

His head hung down, nodding to the soft beat of a song. I recognized it as the one about traveling the world, but that wasn't Dad. He's meant to be alone. My eyes followed his, but he didn't welcome me over. I got the sense I shouldn't get too close to him when his mind was wrapped up in a song. I'd want to stay up later when my Mom called my name for bedtime, but I knew it was time to go. Dad's hug smelled like a smoky fireplace.

When I can't find Dad, he is in the basement trying to cool off since we don't have air-conditioning in the house. The basement is a little cooler, and has a musty, swampy smell. While I look down the dark stairs, as though into a cavern, I could hear his humming to another song on the radio he keeps down there. I raced down the steps, hurrying across the cement floor, past the dark place under the stairs and the frightening corners near the laundry machine. Dad's bushy hair and big glasses made him look like a mad-scientist, more than a crafty carpenter, and his singing makes the basement less creepy.

He's often sitting among the mismatched pieces of a radio he's taken apart, or messing around with the wires of a pair of speakers that he found at a garage sale. I remember my parents talking about the television repair shop in Canastota, New York. I imagined all the television sets, all the VCR's and machinery, that Dad had fixed. His eyes probably fixated on getting the stubborn piece of wire just right. I listened through the grate and heard him recently tell my Mom he was going to build bunk beds soon. I would love bunk beds—I'd get the top bunk, but I've stayed quiet about it.

He had shown me the paperwork for the patent for his invention, the Stop-A-Shock. The name said exactly what it did, stopped a shock from happening. He came up with a way to cover the outlets on the walls so kids couldn't stick things in the socket. It was a small rectangular box that could screw on, over the outlet plate. He got it patented, filed a day before his birthday on February 12th, although it was never manufactured. His eyes prideful as he remembers back, "You were two and half years old, you helped inspire the concept," he said.

"Okay. I got to hear this." Dad turned up the volume up on a radio, the host mentioned a contest coming up to win tickets to the Chiefs baseball game.

The announcer said something about the old movie *The Philadelphia Story* and the actress that played the main character in the musical version of the film. Dad wanted to be the seventh caller and told me about his technique of waiting a beat before calling into the radio station to be the seventh caller and not the sixth.

"Timing is everything," he reminded me.

"Being off by a tenth of a second, could mean a lost opportunity," he said. I stared at his big, spirited eyes, knowing he won't fail.

He had won tickets on the radio many times, from knowing names and dates of films, when things happened and who they happened to, as if he has a catalog of the history of actors in his mind. Last time it was State Fair tickets. Before that it was tickets to the Renaissance Festival.

He was the seventh caller, just like he said he'd be. He used his Shakespearean accent and looked at me while he spoke to the host on the phone. "This is Curtis from Liverpool," he said like they are old friends.

"Why, yes. It is Grace Kelly in *High Society,*" he has on his clever smile.

"A great remake...a lot of great actors in that one," Dad gets more air time going on about Bing Crosby, Frank Sinatra, Celeste Holm, Sidney Blackmer, and Louis Armstrong. He lists the whole cast.

Dad had the answer. He always has perfect timing.

Now I'm only thinking about my time, and my deep breaths of hot air make me thirstier. My arms are lower now, while running against the watch. I hardly have any pump left. My legs clomp, I don't feel as fast anymore. My pace has changed, my legs are starting to tense.

I focus on a yellow patch of grass by what we consider the 300-meter mark, the mark where all the truth creeps in and time starts to move slow. The heat makes me feel grimy, the dirt blackening my ankles. The pat of my feet against the worn lanes are unwilling to drum faster, with the sun scorching my skin.

"Almost there..." Dad shouts over the wide-open field between us. It was faint, but his voice wakes up my muscles up a little. I can't muster up enough energy to yell back, but I rev up my legs. I know every tenth of a second matters. I charge my arms and focus on the final curve ahead. I try to lift my legs a little higher. My calf muscles burn from pushing them so hard. I'm so close. I need to make this last curve count but everything feels cramped up. The sweat is collecting above my eyebrows. Only a little bit more I keep telling myself. I imagine the numbers on Dad's watch rushing by me. This is the final curve to plow through and I can hear Dad calling me. When I reach him, I've made it.

The tendons behind my knees are stiff. I lean my body into the curve, I tell myself to keep my pace—keep my head up, keep stretching my stride, keep my arms high. My arms and fists have become small nudges against the warm air. I want more speed than I can give. The minutes on Dad's watch are rising and I know I'll be slower this time.

Dad's arms are waving me in. "Almost there. Keep going. Don't stop," he yells. He's calling me in, his voice louder as I get closer with more seconds passing on his watch. His face is coming into focus for me. "Come on, Running Rebel, let's go!"

I'm at the last leg of this interval of proving all I've got. My muscles are numb from this rutty track.

"Come on, lift your arms, pump your arms up," he yells louder.

I barely can. The small stones are pinning the backs of my ankles, my shoes clomp into the dirt.

"Come on... keep going...right through, run right past me." He's swishing one arm back and forth as though he had a flag. Through his glasses, his eyes look at me, then look at his watch.

I lean my body forward. I can't feel my legs. I hurl myself right past him, right through Dad's shoe-drawn scrape of a finish line on the dirt.

I hear the beep on his watch.

I fall to the ground, sprawling out in the hot, dried-out grass, gulping breaths of the warm air. The sun in my eyes, my tongue stuck to the roof of my mouth, I heave and gag, thinking I'm going to puke.

"Two point three seconds faster this time, Running Rebel!" Dad says.

The soulfulness in his voice makes me smile, I'm relieved and surprised of myself.

"You're a whole ten seconds faster than when we started out here at the beginning of the summer," he says, helping me up. I've barely caught my breath.

He believes I could be faster than some ninth graders at the high school. I doubt it, but his words make it a possibility. He reminds me that one day I could join a real cross-country or track team. It's a big thought, to run real races, with kids older than me, faster than me, and way ahead of me. Someday, I could go beyond these beat up stomping grounds.

I'm covered in dirt, but I'm suddenly inches taller with an assurance in my heart that the best of me had been seen here. I walk home beside Dad, unnerved, realizing that I'm good at something. I had welcomed the test against time on the track and faced it straight on. Next year I wasn't going to be that girl who cried in class when the pressure to be correct was in the air, or when my classmates finished their tests before me. I know what it feels like to run through the pressure, and I suddenly feel ahead, as though I've learned to run against doubt.

The flicker of Dad's lighter going off makes our time at Zogg feel too fast. Dad will probably go down to the basement to smoke, and he'll want to be alone. From the street we can hear Heidi barking loudly in the back of the house again, and Dad shouts, "quiet Heidi, we're right here." I give her a quick pet before I go inside to get some water and Dad starts wrestling the lawn mower.

Inside, I grab the wallet from the cabinet and hold it carefully. The leather and string have led me to this triumph at the track. It's rugged earth scent, like freshly turned dirt meeting the warm air—even if it had impairments and didn't close shut on its own—held the memories of time together with Dad, and the sound of his voice calling me in during the last longest 100 meters. By curve and straightaway, while on a gritty lane, I had gained my runner legs. I hand the wallet to him back outside and never wanting the summer to end when he put it back in his pocket.

That day will become one of the last times I ran at Zogg. Dad's singing wouldn't last either.

A year later, at the start of the summer before I turned ten, my parents would separate. I would move with Mom and my sister to an apartment complex with newly painted white walls and a clean fresh scent. Gone was the smell of smoke, the smell of Dad. At the green house, I had seen the moon with Dad from the driveway, but now from the balcony of the apartment, all I saw was a black sky.

THANK YOU

I ordered coffee and breakfast pastries and sent it to the firehouse.

I wanted to somehow express their efforts were noticed, some gratitude for being there, I felt a need to say thank you, even though my father had been gone before they arrived.

Pocketknife

Back in Manhattan, two and half months after my father died, I sent my payment of nine dollars and ten cents to the Onondaga County Clerk, with a copy of his death certificate and a letter, asking for any information that was on file under my father's name.

When I read the convictions and sentencings in these files, my shoulders sink and my heart opens more with what has been left unsaid. I'm making peace while staring at these documents that hold the reasons why I hadn't always wanted him in my life. I imagine sitting with him, these records between us and asking, Dad can we please talk about this? Even though we never would.

On the cement patio of my Texas home, I flick open the compartments of my father's pocketknife I found in his car, it reminds me of the one he gave me when I was twelve, and the year that followed —when I wasn't sure I wanted to still care about my father.

The Christmas I was in seventh grade, my father had given me his old pocket knife. The handle is a maroon red, and Dad said he owned it since he was in high school, bought the year before he graduated. It has six compartments, a nail file, small scissors, two blades, tweezers and a screwdriver. It looks like a Victorinox Swiss Army, but it's not. At the bottom of a blade it says it's made in China, a knock-off. Still, there was something valuable about it, and I could tell from the scuffs on the handle and the easy way the blades switched out usefully, that it was a tool with history on it. It was starting to rust and had some grime in the crevices.

I had seen Dad use the nail file, opening bills with one of the small blades, with the other blade cutting the loose ends of tobacco from the cigarettes he now rolled because it was cheaper, the scissors to cut a thin wire while down in the basement. It was icky with crud, it didn't look as though he ever cleaned it. I definitely would've preferred a new pair of running shoes, a journal, or a mood ring. Still, I knew it was a special possession that he had purposely kept, when he took it off of his key ring and handed it to me. I was surprised because he hadn't usually given me a gift at holidays or birthdays. All I had was a small Superman figurine. Now I have a pocketknife.

Although he didn't carve a starting line on the dirt track or time me while running anymore, Dad and I still talked about running when he called Mom's, or when I visited him at our old house. That fall, I ran on the middle school cross-country team with other seventh and eighth graders. We ran a mile and half race first, before the high school Varsity girls took to the course. Dad wasn't a morning person, he said, so he missed most of my races. I forgave him each time and took his encouragement to the starting line.

Once Dad gave me the pocketknife, it was as though our conversations gained more depth, about the boys I was wondering about, how much I hated my glasses and my uncertainty of improving my grades at school. He had the answer, which often included thoughts about the universe. "We are just a sneeze in the creation of all things," he said. Whenever Dad and I had found the North Star, Big Dipper or Little Dipper, he said, "We should always ask what is the purpose of all things." Our brains could connect through energies, he called "brain power." Dad liked to remind me that it was okay to wonder and create my own opinion about whatever I was unsure of. He didn't often mention his childhood to me, besides that he had doubted God since he was about ten years old. His silence about his younger years was like a cue to not bring it up.

I knew he started smoking cigarettes when he was eleven. After he died I'd learn more about the type of teenager he was in an email from his sister, Irene, the one he was closest to, who shared his red hair color. At fourteen, his nickname around his East Syracuse neighborhood was Mad Dog. He could spark at any moment. He would take people on to fight. Mad Dog would often run home as fast as he could with a batch of baked goods under his arm, a morning surprise for his family that he had stolen off a bakery truck. Day-olds, he had said. Only when he got caught, the bakery goods suddenly stopped.

People knew better than to bridle him or confront his philosophies, and he'd often remind his siblings of how smart he was in case they had forgotten. I assume he probably didn't sit still for too long, rolling eyes and feeling bitter, watching the family grow. He was the child who wasn't full-blood. They shared a mother, but he was a part of a previous short-lived marriage, with a different last name than his four half-sisters, half-brother and stepfather.

My grandfather is a ghost of German and English, Irish, and Scot decent. I didn't even know if his name was Francis or Frank. When I had asked Dad about him, he said he barely knew his father, in a matter-of-fact way, the abandonment he experienced surfaced. But then he'd walk away from me, or turn up the volume of the radio and soon I stopped asking about his childhood.

Dad had shared with me a quick story once that he recognized his father's brown shoes, and as a young boy had asked him, "Who are you?" during one of his rare visits. The reply of, "I'm your Dad" didn't hold a fun-loving high-five memory for him that he could share with me.

The short sentences Dad shared about him gave me the impression of someone in a white coat wanting to freeze people's minds and then have the brain come back in time.

I'd learn more about Dad's parents and their relationship from a conversation with his mother, hours after he died. I had been the one to deliver the news about his death to his mother, the grandmother whom I had only received a few birthday cards from.

She was surprised but happy to hear from me, and I imagined her big pretty smile from the few photographs I'd seen of her in my baby book. I began to tremble when I said, "I need to tell you something, about my Dad..." I took a breath as I told her that her son died.

She took a deep gasp that became a scream as she yelled, "He died. My son? My son died!" I started crying with her so hard I could hardly speak. She wailed and screamed over and over. Even though I had already tried to explain, she continued to ask me how this had happened, wanting every detail just like I had from the sheriff.

After a long while, we calmed down. As she talked, it became clear that although I didn't know her well, she had kept a close relationship with my Dad. I wondered if she ever thought about me and why she stayed distant, but I was too afraid to hear the reasons of why she didn't visit or even call. We may have never connected at all, if my father hadn't died. I figured, this was my chance to ask questions about Dad's roots.

She enjoys telling me that although her mother's family was Amish, my great-grandmother Nellie was actually part of the "George White's Scandals." a theatrical entertainment show inspired by the Zeigfeld Follies. I immediately wish I could have met her, and was closer to this side of the family. Then my grandmother says, "Your Dad's red hair is from my father's side."

"Can you tell me something about his Dad?" I asked.

She tells me they met in high school. His father, Frank, was a few years older and played the trumpet and was visiting her school for a concert. She was in a dramatic play. He had said something mundane to her like, "You're the most beautiful girl I've seen" and she gave him some sass saying, "I'd hate to see the others." They dated, got engaged, broke up, and then got back together. When they married it was rocky, especially when she found out she was pregnant. Before Dad was born, his father was getting ready to attend medical school. His mother, nineteen years old at the time, had said something like, "If I get rid of anything, it will be you."

Their marriage would be annulled shortly after my Dad was born. Dad would receive child support checks until he was eighteen. He must have known where his father was living from the address on the envelope, but they didn't communicate beyond that. His father had become a man of science, a doctor, somewhere near Cleveland, Ohio.

His mother opens my eyes to my estranged grandfather, although I only feel a thick wall drawn when I later find his obituary and notice there isn't a mention at all of my Dad.

My grandfather had remarried and had three children, while Dad was placed in a foster home at the age of two, to ease the tension between his mother and stepfather and their five children. Then Dad came back home when he was five years old, where it was crowded and chairs filled quickly. I think of my son Phoenix at only two or three years old, his big grin while he swung on the swings at the playground, and the cuddling when we read a book at night. I cannot fathom how a mother could send her young child away, and how a father could walk away without a word. I'll never know how this abandonment changed my Dad or how deeply it was rooted to his inner nature and state of mind, but I have some ideas.

I can imagine my Dad as a vocal loner who could be quick with a serious boastful opinion or a joke and mockery, but then resort back to his own reclusive space, and his immense comic book collection, of the adventures of Superman, Batman, and The Green Hornet, that he kept locked.

During his sophomore year of high school, he had been involved in a store robbery and with a gang of some sort. That got him into legal trouble and he wasn't yet sixteen when he was sent away from home again, leaving behind his comic books and being Mad Dog. He went to stay with a family who lived and worked on a vegetable farm covering one hundred and thirteen acres in rural Mexico, New York, with full trees separating farm lots, twelve miles away from Lake Ontario.

"Hi, it's Curt's daughter." I'm standing in my kitchen and have an hour before I'll pick up my daughter at her preschool. I turn to a page in my father's high school yearbook with the photo of Julie.

I remember my father pointing out a friend in his yearbook, he said something about living with her family, I couldn't be sure it was the right girl though. I contacted the high school and asked for his transcripts. From them, I see the name on his home address isn't our last name, it's the same last name as Julie.

After some Internet searching and a couple emails later, I hear Julie's easy-going voice on the other end of the phone. She's happy to fill in the blanks although tells me suddenly, "I don't want to say anything that will offend you." I assure her she couldn't.

"I know he had his ups and downs," I say to break the ice.

Julie shares that my Dad was the first foster care child her family had. "He was welcomed to the farmstead, he helped my father with the chores, and my sister and I went to school with him."

A big smile spreads across my face when she says, "My father was warm toward him and would joke and say, 'Come on pumpkin-head,' before they went to do work around the farm. I think he was one of the few male connections your father had."

I listen to Julie's memories of my Dad's red hair and "big eyes that could be a little crazy," she said. I could sense a smile in her voice remembering when he was, "a pain in the ass."

"He liked to tell stories of his city life," Julie reminisces with me about how he enjoyed intellectual conversations about religion and would make statements about the purpose of life that could set a fellow classmate thinking. "Curt had the freedom to be who he wanted. He was no trouble."

She mentioned that he made the champion track team, and of the camaraderie he found there, while in spiked shoes on the track or excelling in the long jump among the close-knit student athletes. In the yearbook I see he joined the school's chorus in the "Swing Wing." I feel proud knowing he was a part of something. He had been a winner of the Regent's Scholarship, a prestigious scholarship based on academic excellence, awarded to undergraduate students in New York State.

"He always had a place to sit here," when she says that I see how the fresh air had given him new ground to root into.

I'm grief-stricken for my father though when she mentions that Dad's best friend Walt, who had ran track with him, had died shortly after high school, from drowning. I would never know how that affected my father, but how could it not? I take my time looking at Walt's picture in the yearbook.

I grab my keys, telling Julie I have to drive to get my daughter but can put her on speakerphone. I'm thankful my Dad had these memories. The change of landscape, farm dust and long grass, had renewed his life—his time in the country allowed him to really run with who he could become. Somewhere between chorus rehearsal, track practices and noticing the moon, he had bought the pocket knife. A souvenir of carving this new path for himself, I believe it was a reminder to him of that marvelous feeling in knowing he did have worth.

Julie tells me he was celebrated at a recent school reunion, and I have tears in my eyes. There had been a ceremony for classmates who had passed away and when she went to get his balloon another friend had

beat her to it. Dad and all his unique charms had been unforgotten in
a place I didn't know had held one of the best times of his life.

After I thank Julie and finally hang up, I sit there in the parking lot of
my daughter's school wiping my eyes and realizing I had been wrong, if
I had gone through with a funeral, the room might not have been close
to empty, like I had thought.

When my parents separated the summer before I turned ten, we
spent two years in the apartment complex near where the road splits in
the village. Then, I had lived with Mom and my sister in the white rental
house back in the village, a one level on Alder Street with a metal fence
around a rose garden; by the cemetery—it was only a few blocks from
our old house.

Dad stayed in our old house during this time. I guess it was Mom's
parting gift to him, that he could stay there, for now. If she didn't pay
the mortgage, he'd probably be homeless. He'd hermit there with Heidi,
the dog my parents had gotten the year before I was born. Apart from
her, he was all alone in our old home. He was back on the porch with
his radio. Or maybe he was out being Mad Dog again. A few days after
Christmas, Dad called. His voice was rushed when he said, "It's just
me."

He sounded furious. His breath heavy. Heidi was told to shut up
and stop barking, and then I could hear him shuffling around, like he
couldn't sit still.

He asked me how I liked the pocketknife. Reminding me it was
sharp, he told me to be careful with it.

I grabbed a note card near the phone while he spoke, I usually drew sketches while I was on the phone. I had written in my loopy cursive "Dad gave me a pocketknife."

He took a deep sigh like he was running his hands through his hair, searching for a smoke and a lighter. As I listened to Dad talk into the receiver, I wrote the word "gas," and put a circle around it.

I wrote "kill myself," then corrected it to "kill himself."

He would kill himself if he lost the house. I wrote while listening to him tell me so casually, with a sneer, a laugh in his words, about how he would do it.

With just a teacher's paycheck, my Mom was having a difficult time paying for both the house mortgage and rent for the new place we were living in.

"Turn on the gas stove," I had written down on the other side of the note card.

"Money sucks."

"No one gets out of here alive."

"Life's a bitch and then you die."

Then, "All he has is the house."

I wrote,"...If die, wanted to live until high school."

He meant me. I would be in high school in another year and half.

I imagined the spit coming out of his mouth as he spoke fast, and laughing with some spite when he said, "Well, I'm going to let Heidi out. I hope I talk to you later."

I held the note card tightly.

"I love you all," he said. Then he hung up before I could tell him that I loved him too. I reread the note card, Dad's words in my hands, and then I hid it under some clothes in the dresser in my bedroom. I believed he loved us too much to really turn on the gas on the stove. He was just having one of his rants about how life is hell, I told myself.

But what if today was different? The uncertainty in my gut was alarming. I imagined him inhaling the gas from the stove, lying on the brown striped couch or the wood floor. I thought of running over there and finding him stiff. If he turned the knob I would be the last person he spoke to. I thought I didn't even have time to run my fastest over to him at the house.

I called him right back, to the phone number that I still knew by heart.

"When the snow melts maybe we can go to Long Branch Park. You can time me running up the big hill," I said. "Remember when you would time me? Or we can go look at moon." I said, even though it was freezing outside.

I could hear his voice soften, "I'll be okay," he said.

That night, I went outside by myself and looked at the moon just like Dad would've normally done. I felt grateful he was alive and at the same time knew he could change his mind in an instant. Then I got in bed and examined the pocketknife, studying each function. The phone at Mom's house did not ring, and I hoped it meant he was just sleeping.

His desire to die stayed with me. I envisioned Dad on the floor, before, during and after my classes at school. Every day I carried the weight of his words. I replayed in my head how he said, "no one gets out of here alive." His disgust for life was only a few blocks away and

I imagined him sitting on the porch alone. I wasn't sure I could keep him alive, even if I ran really well and anyway cross-country wouldn't start again until next year. But I could run to the house in less than three minutes if he needed me. I wanted to suddenly do the math with him on how quick my splits could be if I ran a three-mile race. I called him, but got no answer. I waited for our phone to ring, figuring he'd call when he had a new story to tell about going to hell one day or something else to say.

I wrote his family a letter, "Dear My Family I don't know," writing about how interested I was in knowing them. I never sent it. I'd find it in a box about twenty years later.

Seventh grade hadn't been exceptional for my grades. On my report card it read that I had little respect for authority and I needed to spend more time on homework, I was missing assignments. Mom talked about it with me at dinner time, but I was less interested in what she had to say about my rotten grades. I had my own bedroom for the first time and the small space with a window above my bed was my hideout while listening to music, sketching with colored-pencils, writing poems and practicing to apply mascara and lip gloss.

That spring everything was crumbling fast, a landslide all around Dad. He smoked each cigarette deeply, and only ate a thrown together omelet or a bowl of stale popcorn when I had visited. He looked pale and thin, with a poof of barbaric hair. I didn't want to tell him that I knew how much he wanted to die. Sometimes I would avoid the green house when he called ranting, unsure if being around was better or worse for him, as a reminder of our broken family.

I would be thirteen soon. The summer going into eighth grade I told Dad, "I'm going to meet the high school coach."

Dad reminded me not to let the age difference of the other girls bother me.

I was invited to a summer cross-country practice session at the high school. The girls cheered each other on as they ran, and I tried to stay at the top of the pack. A mile and a half was nothing. I wanted to run three-mile races like them. That day the coach had let me practice with the older girls because he thought I was going into ninth grade, and I was so disappointed later when he said I couldn't train with them just yet.

Although I was short, I presented myself as strong and perceptive to the world. My new maturity meant I'd attracted the attention of boys. It was around this time that Mom caught me with a boy I liked in my bedroom when I thought she wasn't home. I had broken her rule about boys at the house. We jumped out my bedroom window. I refused to go back to our house, and that evening I went to Dad's. Back in my old bedroom, I crawled up on the top bunk of the never-used bunk beds he had made us after my parents separated. I deeply inhaled the smell of the wood mixed with the dusty and smoky air from Dad's cigarettes, the comforting smells of my childhood.

I planned to never go home to Mom and to instead live with Dad. I had never stayed with him. I saw him in spurts, an hour here, a look at the moon together, a visit to help him rake leaves or shovel snow, but I had never stayed with him for consecutive days. As I drifted off to sleep, I thought, I could live here. It would be Heidi, Dad and me, sitting among the pale green walls of the dining room that used to make me think of mint chocolate chip ice cream. Ever since he gave me the pocketknife and called me about wanting to die, a deeper comradery was built between us. Except I wanted him to live and he wanted to die. He would live to see me graduate high school, I told myself.

Dad didn't give me rules. I told him about the boy I liked who had jumped out the window with me, and he warned me that I had plenty of time, and that boys usually talked less than girls and if I didn't hear from him not to worry too much. We threw the ball high in the air to see how high Heidi could jump and catch it in her mouth. I sat with him, while he smoked cigarettes, he was blowing the smoke away from me even though I didn't mind it, and even sang with him. I let his cravings go, he could drink it all. I snapped my fingers along as he sang the song "Cool Jerk" and added his name to it as Cool Curt.

While I noticed how empty the fridge was, I suddenly wondered what happened to his job at the television repair shop in Canastota, and his invention of Stop-A-Shock, when he was worried about electrical outlets and my small hands—but his ideas had become a short-circuit.

When we all lived together, I wasn't supposed to touch the answering machine or the phone in the dining room that Dad never answered. I heard his voice recording every time people called about College Resource Services. He finished his personal voice message with his signature, "And, goodbye for now." Like narrator ending the last scene of a play.

Dad hardly checked the answering messages anymore. "That business was just a get-rich-quick scheme that didn't work out," he said when I asked about it. The house he had rented out on 6th street, when my parents were together, turned out to be another loan they lost money on and "was too expensive to maintain," he said. I wasn't sure his latest gigs selling newspaper subscriptions was his best option but couldn't guess what would be.

He went to the porch. His voice that once so truly pulled me home from the final curve of the dirt track, was faithless. The emptiness in Dad's eyes was starting to get to me. After five days I began to wonder if I should leave. I was getting hungry for more than omelets and popcorn. I called Mom to see what she and my sister were doing, apologizing for breaking her rules and jumping out the window. A little school shopping with Mom sounded like the perfect exit. Laying on the top bunk in the darkness, I listened for a creak, for his footsteps stumbling to the couch downstairs, but Dad stayed up late smoking on the porch. He slept deep into the morning, and I tapped him on the shoulder, but as I expected he was too deep in drunken sleep and did not wake up. I left.

One Saturday afternoon soon after, Dad asked if I could babysit for a friend of his, who lived a few blocks away, while he went out with her that night.

I agreed to babysit. I liked the idea of pocket money, but didn't know I'd be there so late. As the night wore on, I kept rocking the baby, who had fallen asleep. I heard someone struggling to put their key into the house door. Dad's friend rushed in, her legs were as skinny as a bird, and she didn't look like she just had a newborn baby. I was relieved she was back, I didn't want to watch such a small infant any longer.

"I'm not in the mood to see your father anymore tonight," she said reaching for her baby.

"He'll be here in a minute though." She sounded annoyed. "Tell him I'm still out." Then she handed her sleeping baby back to me and a handful of rumbled dollar bills and disappeared to the dark part of the house in the back.

I didn't want to be the messenger. I wanted to go back home and to my bed. I was hoping Dad would come back soon and I could leave. When he got there, he didn't try to see if the door was locked and just busted through, with a gust of familiar stench tagging along.

I rocked the baby who had woken at the sound of the door slamming. "Did she come back yet?" he asked. He leaned against the wall. His eyes were bulging.

"No. Not yet." I said, looking down, hushing the baby, and in the hush I held my lie.

"I swear she left. Maybe she's still there." Dad's thoughts were restless and rattling. His slurred words about being a fool, running his mind around being there, not being there, going back, and repeating himself.

His eyes went from ceiling to floor, to the door, trying to remember what had happened. "She's probably with someone." He didn't want to go back out, but was too upset to stay.

I told him I was tired.

"I'll be back soon," he said, ignoring my desire to go home.

His mouth was drooling some as he lit a cigarette and took a long drag, then turned to go, and straightened up the collar on his coat, telling me again he wouldn't be long.

He looked back at me, noticing the baby in my arms.

"You used to be that small."

"Smaller"

"A peanut."

He left.

I slung into the couch to wait, believing he'd be right back.

The woman was quiet in her room behind me. The baby was quiet too.

I didn't want to be there any longer. I gave up on waiting on him. I gave the sleeping baby back to the woman and ran to Mom's house. I ran under the street lights, dashing through the darkness of 5th Street, and was extra careful at Oswego Street waiting for traffic, with each pump of my arms I pushed away the worry for where Dad was. He had ditched me.

As soon as I got home, I tucked my blankets over my head like a sheath to forget into. I let Dad's slurred words go, his wobbling, the boozy smile that had absorbed my lie. He could capsize and collapse somewhere. I was tired of caring and being there. He probably would pass out, and walk home in the morning from where he landed, hung over and staggering. I'd hear from him soon, I thought.

Mom had shared in a sigh the next day that Dad had gotten into some trouble. I didn't want to upset her or ask more questions, and I wasn't sure I wanted the answers anyway.

The phone was quiet for a week or so until he called to tell me about the moon phase. He didn't mention the dreadful night I had babysat for his friend. Maybe he had been too wasted to remember. I had found out that after he left that night, he hadn't kept his car on the right half of the road on the way back to the bar. He had been pulled over and was charged with driving while intoxicated. The law had changed since his earlier DWIs, and now it only took two DWI convictions within the preceding ten years to be given a felony charge. This one joined with a previous charge on file would work against him.

On the phone with him, he only wanted to talk about me, what I had been up to and how my last cross-country race had gone. I told him the season was ending soon. We talked about the moon, I remembered in my baby book his baby name ideas for me had included Imogene, meaning an image, and Selena meaning the moon. If I had been a boy, there was the name Derk Cosmo. Our conversation was brief but he sounded okay.

During another conversation, though, he was agitated. By then, he knew word had gotten out about his DWIs. Swearing, he said his court date wouldn't be until the spring.

The next day I went to school sleepy-eyed, worrying if he was still having suicidal thoughts. As my eighth-grade cross-country season ended, I was included in the morning announcements. When I heard my last name over the school's intercom, Dad's last name, the night I babysat flashed before me. His slurred words and wobbly stance, him being pulled over, showing his ID, his arrest, his solitude, how I didn't really know him at all, made my heart trip up. The dirt track felt forever ago. I walked the halls with my head down. It felt as though my classmates could see right through me.

That winter I decided not to tell him my news on winning a Gold Key Art award. I knew Dad's license was suspended and he couldn't get to the ceremony at Oswego College himself, the same college town where he and Mom had first met each other at a bar many years ago. I didn't want to touch upon the detachment between my parents now.

The art teacher had submitted my mixed media piece of overlapping Volkswagen Beetle shaped cars, to a regional contest sponsored by the Alliance for Young Artists and Writers. Four thousand and eight hundred pieces of art were submitted, Dad, I wanted to tell him. I was one of a handful of 8th graders in Central New York to win! He would've liked that part. But I didn't bother. I had turned a quick sketch of these old junky cars into an award that was stamped with a gold emblem on the border. I had art and I had running, and no one in that audience knew my Dad had another DWI.

In the spring, with my ear to the phone while letting Dad talk about his lack of electricity and cigarettes and his headaches, he said, "I might have to spend some time in the slammer," a little too coolly.

"It takes money to be free." He was mad at the laws. I didn't fully believe he'd spend time in prison, even though he didn't have the money to pay the sentencing fines of two-thousand and five hundred dollars, along with a mandatory surcharge of one hundred and fifty dollars.

Dad had sighed, "...Well, it's five years' probation and the first six months to be served at Jamesville Wasteland." He meant Jamesville Correctional Facility.

He told me not to worry too much, he was going to appeal the convictions and fines, and would go to trial again sometime next fall, when I started ninth grade.

You caused this, I wanted to tell him. This was the life you chose. I was tired of being the only one who cared about why his world was running on empty. It took more than the right posture of arms high on a dirt track to get ahead. It took hard work and drive. It took commitment. He'd taught me that. Why didn't he see it for his own life?

I wanted to be in ninth grade already. I clung to the thought of running cross-country with the high school team next fall. Time could not move fast enough. Mom also wanted a new start. She moved us from the rental we were in, to a different house, five miles away from where my Dad was. I would be done with my eyeglasses bouncing on my face too, with contact lenses soon. A fresh start on a new course. I would be ready with my new training shoes on. Dad could be serving time, but I'd be running.

I suddenly didn't care if he ever saw me run again. I would leave his words of regret in the dust behind me. If he wanted to die and would be happier, then maybe he would be better off, I said to myself.

In school, the 78 grade point average I started with the first marking period had dropped to 73, but it didn't faze me. One day I just walked out of French class when I didn't know the answer. I missed a lot of assignments in Social Studies and couldn't get past a C in English. I kept in mind the words to a poem I had written during the winter about my father, *I claim him because he is the only one I have. Not my choice. Part of my Life.*

I held tight to my refusal to call him back as eighth grade was ending. In a few weeks I wouldn't be able to run in-between my parents' homes anymore. Soon I'd be away from him, and his felony would be behind me.

As I began packing, I saw the pocketknife in my dresser drawer. I thought about Dad using it. The past couple years had been hard on my backbone, I didn't want to stand by him anymore.

The landline rang. I wasn't sure I wanted to be the one who answered the phone. The pocketknife went in a box, taped up. I rolled my eyes at the phone and its constantly ringing. It had been easy to delete his messages before, and I'd do it again.

This message caught me off guard though.

I could hear my father's voice talking into the answering machine, getting to the point quickly, he spoke in a whisper as though he was holding back tears, losing his breath in his grief-stricken words. Heidi had died.

My cold shoulders dropped. I didn't want to care, but I did. He had said I didn't need to come, but I ran over as fast as I could.

I bet myself I could get to the green house in less than three minutes. If I pushed it and if there wasn't much traffic to wait for at Oswego Street, even less. I sprint down the sidewalk of 5th Street. The almost-summer breeze on my cheek and my enormous glasses bouncing on my nose as I ran. I curved right into the long driveway, passing the window-enclosed porch at the front of the house, my arms pumping just like I had at Zogg.

Dad was standing by the big maple tree, near the garage at the back of the house. He had a red shovel in his hand. His loyal Heidi had gotten sick and gone. I saw Heidi's black and brown fur, her eyes closed as Dad covered her up. I didn't say a word while I caught my breath. I wanted to pet her goodbye but it was too late. At least I had made it before Dad's last shovel of dirt went over her.

I thought of Heidi scratching at her fleas down to her skin, I remembered Dad's message saying before that she had been limping. She had known Dad longer than I had. Heidi was the binding connection he had to our family. There would be Heidi for him to tell us about on the phone. She was a reminder of togetherness. Now as dirt went over Heidi, I held back from rolling my eyes at him, disgusted by how the paint of the green house was peeling off and flaking away, and the yard had been forgotten and filled with weeds.

Dad couldn't take care of us or give us his share. He couldn't repair televisions, or invent another thoughtful invention like Stop-A-Shock. He couldn't get a loan or pay the electric bill this month. He was uncombed, unshaven and had dirt under his nails. He didn't show up at any of my races. He couldn't drive since he had lost his license, and is probably is going to jail. He couldn't take care of me. Dad didn't have any more words to share on the moon or the meaning of human existence.

When he had given me the pocket knife it was something he considered a keepsake I could grow into. But it only revealed facets of his life that I wasn't proud to stand by. Since then, he told me he wanted to die, he had smelled boozy every time I saw him, and I had grown tired of his stories of how much life is hell.

I wasn't sure I wanted it anymore. I couldn't remember the last time we had laughed together. Dad just wanted to die, and I stood there thinking maybe he should. I started to search for what I'd miss about him, while convincing myself I didn't need his grimy pocket knife. I decided I'd throw it out when I got back home.

"Living fourteen years is very long for a dog," Dad says while holding the shovel still. I would be fourteen that fall.

"She was a sister to you." His voice got softer. "You and your sister were her puppies. She taught you how to walk. You would hold her fur to stand."

Dad tossed the last of the soil over Heidi's body and wiped tears from his eyes. I stayed quiet while he patted the ground.

I understood why his head hung low to a soft beat and I wasn't sure I wanted him in my life. I looked around the yard to the driveway where mom's car used to be parked, through the bushes of the neighbor's house, and I could see where Dad and I had run.

I didn't know back then I'd be standing here now with Dad, just five years later, unsure of the place he held in my life. I focused on the mound of dirt in front of me. Then how our best memories had also ended with dirt.

I stood there unsure that he would ever be the father I wanted. I comprehend the loss of my childish imagining of who he was that had been short-lived. As he buried my childhood dog, I knew that he would never show up and be the type of father I wished he was at the sidelines of my life. Standing beside him as he stared at the ground, I would have to let go of who he wasn't and what never would be, to carry him on in my life. Something told me I didn't want to lose him, but I also didn't know what I'd gain by sticking around.

My best races were in front of me, I'd see who I'd really become while staring down the future whether he was there or not. No matter what life brought, there would be an opportunity for a comeback. I could trip and stumble, lose my pace and place. I could also get myself back on track, I could run through it all without him, and I could show up again. This, I wanted to believe.

I decided to hold onto the pocket knife to prove that a new beginning would be there. I thought about Dad buying it, and I try to find my way through the intricate maze of who he was back then, and the dead-end before him now. For all his hits and misses, there had to be another comeback for him, and he would see that his life had worth.

The door to walk away was wide open.

The mound of dirt about to close up my heart. But I stepped in closer.

I'd be there.

I'd be the one standing by.

I'd be his family.

I would listen.

I would care.

I reached for his hand. Dad's hands were dirty, soiled from patting the ground down and his eyes were swollen red. "I've got to get out of this heat," he said while wiped his eyes with his shirt. His pants hung low on his waist as though he'd lost some weight. I noticed gray strands in his hair. I stayed there for a little longer looking at the mound and the shovel Dad had left next to it.

Nearby, Without a Goodbye

When my children were smaller, I would keep my father's urn in their shared bedroom. To their young eyes, they may have thought the urn was just a wooden box with a mountainous landscape carved into it. To me, it was a comfort to somewhere have him present in their lives, as though my dad could get a chance to experience their joy, squeals of excitement while they grew and toddled around with toy trains and balanced blocks.

New Testament

I was surprised to find a New Testament in Dad's car. He had written his name on the inside. I don't know how long he's had it for, and I wonder how often he turned the pages, or if he had remembered a verse when he needed to ease his mind, maybe he repeated the words under his breath.

There's a church in Phoenix, New York, The First Congregational United Church of Christ. Dad told me about going there in the months before he died. I picture him praying there.

A week after my fourteenth birthday, Dad had his trial and pled guilty to drunk driving as a felony. He will attempt to appeal the sentence, he says during a quick phone call, but he would still spend at least four months at Jamesville.

The following week I won the cross-country race at Rome Free Academy against Oswego and Cicero–North Syracuse High School. I don't tell anyone on my team that my father is in prison.

Two weeks after Dad went to prison, I have another race. I made a mark, placing 6th out of one hundred and three runners at the Auburn Invitational. My name made the newspaper for that race. Each week I had finished mostly in a top ten spot.

With my new contact lenses, I see the full horizon across courses all over the Central New York area. I have to beat my best time. I have new goals to reach, I wrote them down, and I run hard toward them. I feel strong at the front of the pack through the season. I try not to think of Dad too much, although he is there on my mind at every sound of the starting gun and beep on the watches of officials and coaches, every time my foot hits the dirt path. I breathe in deep the cool fall air. My feet pounding the hills, wearing the course on my ankles, through mud and sleet. I train all week for this race. My race is where I give the best of me.

While Dad is in prison, I give myself to a boy that cross-country season.

I fall hard for him, but he is just another thing to lose. The place I feel any certainty and purpose is when I'm with my team and running. I have my ribbons on a tacked board in my room that remind me of that spirit and unity. I try to forget about what I've lost.

That fall and into winter Dad wrote letters to me, my sister and Mom from prison. Some were written on lined paper, as though ripped out of a notebook. His large writing fit the lines from top to bottom. A profound word could get two capital letters in a row to start it off. Then his writing could become looping cursive the next word, all caps the next, written all the way to the edge, not wasting a space to share how he was doing, each sentence looks spilled out of him. The letters were the first time he had mentioned talking to a reverend and about praying and Jesus in a way that was hopeful and full of belief. His words on the page as though a bridge toward forgiveness.

Jamesville Correctional Facility

C-B Inmate Number: 8700-1642

Dear Girls,

The first real snow fell today and stayed on the ground all day. It's always lonely here but the snow deepens our individual and collective isolation.

I've got probably 7 or 8 more weeks here, and each day passes slowly without much to look forward to, except more of the same old shit. There are programs here, but due to budget cuts, fewer are effective or really productive. I'm still going to computer school but it's a slow and deliberate process, etc., etc.

Let's face it, we are all here for punishment and to perpetuate a failed social system. Two thirds of the people here would have benefited more by weekend incarceration, halfway houses or community services. "Alternatives to Incarceration" the non-violent, so-called victimless "crimes" which in reality are moral choices rather than outright crime. I do realize however that I will have to change if I don't want to come back here. I will need social services first and then a "real" job. Maybe I can help change this "system" which I and most of us so abhor. I should be grateful I'm still as healthy as I am. I weigh about 160lbs (not all fat either) but could be in even better shape if I made the effort.

Thank you for those messages; they keep me from dwelling and stressing about it.

I miss cigarettes, it's not easy to quit, they (cigs) are around but it's not easy to get them and the penalties are worse than in Junior or Senior High

School. Speaking of Junior High some of the people here have difficulty understanding Sesame Street, no shit it's sad and a little scary.

They should separate us by sanity level, and IQ, or even age, but that would cause less problems for the C.O.s and they'd be arguing about who or why they got punished or not "privileged" to work with the less disruptive prisoners. Girls I'm sorry if my being in here has embarrassed you. I really didn't think after 8 1/2 years of good driving and no other charges I'd wind up here in the Jamesville Wasteland.

The sunsets are beautiful as are the surrounding hills. I think about all of you almost constantly, and it's not easy "being" here. I worry about you; don't rebel yourself into juvenile delinquency as I did. Do as I say and not as I do, you bet. I never ever want to see you in a place like this, your too sweet, kind and beautiful for that.

Both of you could read "Little Girl Lost," by Drew Barrymore with Todd Gold 1990, youngest of a long line of great and rebellious actors and actresses.

It's time to "Get a Life" as Howard Stern says on 95X. I still want to help people; maybe to not come here or to a worse place, and there are worse places, I know that. If I can ever make up for the sadness and embarrassment this time has caused us all. I will, I definitely will, at least try, maybe you all can try to forgive me as I will have to forgive myself to get a better life for me and you; all of you.

With love that binds Dad/Curt

On the margins of the letter he's hoping we will write soon.

With another P.S. telling us he had been praying and that, it seems to help, "it definitely doesn't hurt," and he included that we should try it.

He asks for boots in another P.S. ...*like my brown ones, Salvation Army maybe you can buy my old ones back ha ha.*

He asks for batteries, *always appreciated.*

He thanked Mom for the $10.00 commissary and wrote that he would need more in there soon.

A day later he had written again.

Saturday 2:20 p.m. C-B sec.

Inmate Number 8700-1642

Dear Girls,

I've started my 14 day lock-in here at B-A house. I was here a few weeks ago. At least they have a T.V. I can stare down at from my cell. I went to small yard recreation, 8:30 AM, by myself, walked around an enclosed area but could breathe fresh air and see sunny blue skies even though it was a little chilly this A.M.

I went to church and heard a duet by the Reverend and another Inmate. It was very well done and sang of communion with Jesus. I do pray here; you really must to not feel too alone, among the many others who seem O.K but are deeply saddened by this prison. Please visit me again soon as you can. Sunday or Monday through Thursday. I'm proud of my girls for doing so well in school.

He wrote to me specifically...*if you can average C's or better you'll be OK; 9th grade is very hard for all students growing up socially and academically.*

To Mom he writes: *If you need for me to sign the check let my counselor know. $1000 or so (split of $1,940 would help me get started all over again (Tracy Chapman song). I don't ever want to be back here. Pick up P.A forms in Syracuse and send them to me when you can. I love you all with all my heart.*

Love, Curtis/ Dad

In the margins of the letter it reads:

P.s I still could use some boots but don't go crazy looking for them, a plain not gray sweatshirt and sweatpants, no pockets.

... The days grow short when you reach November and December but get longer and brighter in January and February

...I can help with your problems in school or out, even people here sometimes appreciate my advice or thoughts on their problems.

...Keep running track and C.C. your as good as any of the others, show them. Did you find the book Little Girl Lost by Drew Barrymore?

I have never been baptized, I didn't grow up with crosses displayed on the walls or routinely attend church or Sunday school. The way Dad wrote about Jesus in the letter was new. I imagine him praying, beside the reverend. Until these letters, he only spoke of going to hell and life being a bitch and then you die. Through the pen, I find hopefulness and belief, the kind of Dad I always wanted to have.

When I asked, Mom took me to see him in prison. We went through the long wait and the thick doors, and I noticed the serious eyes of security guards watching and listening to our conversation during the short visits. Mom sat quietly while I talked to my Dad. My sister was probably too scared to speak much. Dad's smile seemed scripted and overworked as he asked us questions about how we were doing. Face to face in the large visiting room, he had less to say that was new, and repeated much of what he had already written in his letters, and how he was going to be there for us when he got out. I wanted to believe him.

I didn't hold the memory of visiting him in jail too close, or want to remember sitting with him there, dressed in an inmate uniform, while being confined and restricted from our lives.

November 17 11:30 a.m.

A House #3

Dear Girls,

Well I've finally been transferred to A house. Where the so-called "hard cases" go. I was really not bothering anyone. It was very very good to see you both if only for 12 1/12 minutes; thirteen if you count goodbyes. I must do 12 days in here, it's in a cell with toilet and a sink, good lights above, about 7 1/2 feet by 12 feet long, 8 feet high. The inmates in here are crazy; they've lost their focus on reality and are involved with small details of an abnormal and boring environment. "Jail is jail." I don't ever want to come back here again. I've taken mild sleeping medication, but ignorant loud mouthed louts are everywhere. I call it "The Noise." They are psychopathic, psychotic personalities, externally, selfish and childish.

It will be remarkable if I make it during this period of punishment, for punishment sake. It's just a waste of precious time, but it can get better, here and for me. I was doing ok until a sadistic petty minded rat like, snake C.O decided to ruin me; they are attracted to controlling and mind screwing inmates. It's really not a pleasant job but etc, etc.

I'll look very much forward to all letters, short or long even post carols during this time. I bet they took your (my) magazines, I never got them. I hope the ride home was ok. I really needed to see you both. I miss you terribly, sometimes so sadly, I lose it and cry. But even the "tough" guys cry sometimes. Send or bring me a sweatshirt, boots etc, etc, "life is an illusion, we must re-create each day."

Love you all, Curt/Dad

I wasn't sending Dad letters back too often. I had cross-country training every day until dinner time and could hardly keep up with my homework, let alone write him a letter that he'd read while in a cell in prison. I didn't want thinking about him to always be a part of my day.

There are messages on the answering machine from Dad, and when we speak on the phone he talks about himself, how many weeks he had left, something the reverend at the correctional facility had told him about forgiveness. I draw on a pad of paper, only half listening during his calls, or ask him a question about my math homework.

I hope you like this card it only cost 65 cents including postage. I'm sure you've written by now. It's about 3:30 pm, I may still get a letter. You see I was in B-A house for two days Friday night till Sunday. Then here so perhaps your letters were returned or you just didn't have time to send them. I'll have only 43 days left here after you receive this card. 1 month and 1 week; so not forever but it seems like eternity. I'll have been sober for almost 9 months when I get out and want to do something important with the rest of my life. If I live to grandpa's age I've got almost 30 years left and people are doing more as they get older, who knows what science will develop in the next 5-10 years. Maybe we can all live more productive lives.

Reverend got me a good pair of sneakers; now a decent pair of winter boots would go far. Although beauty is in the eye of the beholder and love has no pride, the bonds we have with our children are more beautiful when love is unconditional, and forgiving.

He mentioned friends that might call and that it was okay to share his inmate number with them.

...We are all alone here together, together alone, but alone together.

...Ask Mom to write. Where's your report card girls (copy)?

...When your thinking of me, I'm thinking of you, and if the phone doesn't ring it's me! Ha Ha Sleep well and pleasant dreams.

With all my love, Dad, Curtis

That winter, Syracuse University's Manley Field House smells of rubber, and the air is dry and warm. I inhale it deep when I walk into the arena with my high school indoor track team for weekly meets with other Central New York high school runners.

Because the coach knows me, and has seen me train with the high school girls, I've jumped up to Varsity for the distance and middle-distance races. This is my first indoor season competing with the high school track team, finally. I'm the only freshman running Varsity this indoor track season, and I'm pushing myself so much to keep my spot, improve my time, stay right there in sync with the junior and senior leaders on the team.

I walk into the arena trying not to make eye contact with the competition, holding my track bag, with my homework and racing flats tucked inside. My hair is pulled up into a tight ponytail, and my feet already jittery and ready to move faster. I have on my orange shorts and my uniform tank top with Liverpool on my chest. I walk with the older girls on my team as their sidekick. They inspire me to want even more from myself, their words cheering for me fill up a part of me that is empty and their voices call me into the last stretch of my race. We park our bags right outside the first curve of the track. There's homework to do before warming up for my race. I try to focus on math, which I'm struggling with. I need to keep a 70 average to run on the team.

I put on my favorite pink lip gloss before my race, it's my trademark and I never go without it. My jersey is so big I wrap the straps around my sports bra straps with a twist to hold the name Liverpool up higher on my chest. On the track while standing in runner position and waiting for the gun to go off I shake off any missteps at my back. When I blast off I try not to notice the fathers cheering on their daughters at the side of the track with words of encouragement. I know I'm not only trying to run ahead of the others but with each step I'm leaving behind me a piece of my father and the parts of him I cannot change. When I feel the burn in my legs it's as though each stride is a chance to create my own identity and running is my lucky break free from the stumbling blocks in my life. My heart soars and I'm enclosed with comfort and dignity when I cross the finish line breathless.

The last letter I have from Dad is marked for December 24th and it's really directed to me.

I realize you are going through a difficult time. So am I honey, so am I. After all these years of trying to change and get a life its past time now to try and make amends. Maybe I can work in area of social work that helps people. There are councilors here who have gone through the same problems I have and are now working for places, like this (Jamesville) and other types of Social Services.

How is your rebel thing going? I'll bet you don't like being told what to do either. By the time you get this I'll have only 16 more days left. I get out 12:01 Am January 8th. I'll need a ride for I'll have a lot of junk, clothes, radio, books, shoes, boots etc. It's amazing what you can accumulate in less than four months. Maybe Mom can pick me up after school and take me somewhere, then I could visit you. I won't have a car or a license but could rent a house and go to meetings and councilors at the Syracuse Veterans Hospital for counseling 1 hour per week. I know I'm a little bit old to be in counseling but at least I'm alive and able to help others with the help of Jesus. Jesus or what men call Christ does exist in the hearts of men. Sometimes it's all too easy to forget that and "run with the devil." I will at least try to never come back here. I want to help the family in any way I can but first must be responsible for myself.

I'll (always) love you girls with all my heart. Dad (Curtis)

I imagine Dad waiting outside the correctional facility in early January, a little past midnight, the air chilly and wind against his face, his belongings disheveled in his arms. He's free, but stuck waiting for his ride from a friend to pick him up. Standing there, he might've looked up at the night sky above him, thinking about his next steps and the words in the scripture he needed to keep his heart aglow. Prison had given Dad the gift of faith, the newfound belief, carried throughout his life, that he too could be forgiven.

GRIEF SONG

I played Songbird by Fleetwood Mac while I picked out my father's urn. It was a day after he died. I didn't originally like the song, the sorrowful lyrics and each word stretched in a coo and moan, about wishing someone all the love in the world, but the song became my grieving song, it was perfect. I later placed the urn on the coffee table and played the song on repeat.

GIANTS HAT

Dad's Giants hat was squashed under a cardboard box of pantry items, when I found it in his car. I had seen him wear it during a visit to Syracuse a few years ago. It's stained as though dunked in dirty water or commuted daily and worn against the heat, rain, snow and wind during his walk from his home to the car, making his way to the gas station down the road. On the brim there are stitches of thread, where he had tried to sew the edges of the hat back together.

Holding the hat now, it reminds me of a similar hat my father had worn to a couple of my track meets in high school. I'm unsure if the one in the car was the exact hat from back then, but it looks old enough to be.

One of my last memories of my father involves this exact hat. It was a few years before he died.

He was wearing this stained hat when I got out of the rental car with my then-boyfriend. I was home although standing on the main street of my childhood in the village of Liverpool, the small park with the fountain to my right, where I watched concerts and danced to my parent's oldies music, the bank across the street, my first bank, the library and the circulation desk where I checked out a stack of books that went over my head, the shoe cobbler and cobblestone streets near some antique stores to my left, a lakeside small grocery store, where I once stole a few diapers for my dolls, a crisp fall breeze coming off Onondaga lake, and golden and maroon maple leaves on the sidewalk, although unseen in the photo of my father and I that day. Standing there, the village existed just the same as my father's gray hair hidden by the hat.

He wore an American flag pin on his blazer, paired with a white two pocket shirt. His big glasses seem to cover half his face. He looked good with his face shaved, holding a leather portfolio I had bought as a gift for a birthday.

When we hugged hello his smokey scent reminded me of living in the green house and our walks to Zogg to run. I was wearing my favorite dangling earrings, a pair from the Metropolitan Museum of Art Store at Rockefeller Center and a cropped silk jacket. It made me feel elegant and eccentric at the same time. Dad might have mumbled something about how I was a city girl now when I introduced him to my boyfriend. It was only two and a half blocks down Tulip street and we were there by the marina and boat launch. I doubt he mentioned where he was living or much about himself. A part of me wanted to ask questions about his life, maybe he would share a story about his younger years, but a stronger pull in my heart kept me quiet. The choppy waves and the big boats and the pretty white paint of the yacht club building took over my wonders, my hair was windblown when we settled on a new wooden bench by the marina.

Since I left for college, there hadn't been much quality time between us. If I visited the Syracuse area, I would go to my mom's house to devour spaghetti and meatballs, and have conversations about movies, books and city life. If I saw my father, we met at the train station for a short visit on my way back to the city. So this walk and carved out time with him is new, it must have been planned as a detour before hitting the road at the end of the trip.

Dad started talking about lakeside memories. "At the Lakefront Extravaganza the lead singer of the oldies band The Platters shook her hand during a song and she didn't let go so he pulled her up on stage." I sang along for the rest of the song, I was probably three or four years old. I have no memory of this but I have heard this story from Mom too.

He mentions us riding bikes to the marina when we lived in the green house. It might have been less than an hour to bike there and back but it felt like an adventure zipping down the sidewalks of the tree-lined streets named after trees. From Fifth street we could go down Birch, Bass or Balsam to the scenic view of the blue lake above the trees blending into the sky until we got closer, past the library and bank, and antique shops, zooming down a hill, and the land leveled, the water struck the rocks at the shore. We'd park bikes and sit on a bench and if he had a Snickers candy bar in his coat pocket he'd split it with me, we'd chew the caramel, peanuts, and chocolate and then bike back. Dad's hat kept the sun out of his eyes and near the lake his smokey smell wasn't as strong, his thirst for a drink was less, he was occupied with the horizon and his eyes focused on where the land and water met.

Suddenly I wished one of us had brought a Snickers to the lake.

During one of our bike rides I must have asked about a white patch of land across the lake. Dad said we could bike to it. It was the longest ride. As we biked, Dad was singing a tune about blue skies and nothing being in our way, and when we passed the two big boulders our bikes just fit through the space between them, and we whipped down the hill to the lake. I liked to fly down to the pathway not using my brakes fully, my banana seat bumping my butt.

Dad was ahead, steering one handed, while smoking a cigarette. The sun was blazing down, the long branches of the willow and chestnut trees reflecting in the water, as we biked by Willow Bay and my bike streamers rustled as we passed kids at the wooden playground and metal slate slide, and when the trolley went by we waved.

I peddled and pushed on. We had gone about two miles. "We are halfway already," Dad said. We were on a new path toward the West Shore of the lake, a jungle, terrain I've never biked over before, with branches blocking our way, whacking our arms and legs as we peddled on. Passed a splash of a turtle or aquatic life bustling midday, racing with a flock of birds rising from the shoreline. Through the trees I could see the lake's rippling water. My arms got tired of holding the handlebars, my legs were aching from cycling, but I didn't want to stop.

We peddled through tall grass and suddenly white ground appeared. A beach. The sand wasn't fluffy, it was flaky, but we had made it.

From there, across the lake I could see the square shape of the boathouse and the white yachts at the marina, homes in the village looked like dots against the village trees.

When Dad looked out at the lake, he exhaled his cigarette into the soft wind.

"Is this really a beach?" I asked.

Dad took a long drag of his cigarette, "It probably was." A chemical company that produced soda ash, meant for soaps, baking powders and detergents, dumped their waste in the lake, he explained. People are the eyes of nature, it was up to us not to ruin it, but it already was contaminated, my father said slowly. I knew he bought cartons of cigarettes at the Onondaga Reservation, "it's cheaper," he said. I imagined the Iroquois, the Haudenosaunee, meaning People of the Longhouse, and their high ceiling homes, symbolic as the sky, and the dirt floor below as mother earth, an opening at the very top for cooking fire smoke to escape. The Haudenosaunee were standing at the edge of this lake making peace on the shores with the Mohawk, Onondaga, Oneida, Cayuga, and Seneca nations. As Dad spoke about how dirty the water was, I wanted to gather sticks for their fires, sit braiding grass with them in silence and grieve their sacred and now polluted lake.

I wanted to ask why we were biking to a polluted lake, and what was the point of bike rides to a place that had garbage at the banks and sewage discharge and contamination at the bottom and stunk, and I wanted to leave. The birds flew along the toxic shoreline, and the dragonflies resting on wetlands flourished with residue, the frogs, turtles and fish that made a home on the lake were tricked and threatened. The salt marshes and surrounding watergrass with poison in its veins.

The journey back was slow. I biked with a stern steady pace, not pushing too hard, glancing at the lake through the brush. Dad said I was the youngest person to bike that far when we reached the village and the two big boulders.

"It's still a beautiful lake. Look." He said pointing out to the water. The sun had started to go down, the sun shimmered on the lake making it sparkle, its imperfections below the surface, a reflection of orange and pink was beaming behind us as we reached the village. After he died, I would have an impulse to memorialize him and order a bench from Onondaga Lake Park in his memory to be placed by the marina.

Sitting on the bench with him and immersed in youthful recollections, I didn't know he was going to die a few years later, I would have asked for more stories, more of his reflections and time. When his eyebrows rose up under the brim of his hat when he called me The Running Rebel, it was expected to hear a line up of accolades.

He started to brag about how quick of a runner I once was. I could only remember a couple times my father had shown up at my high school races. I let him go on about my running stats to my boyfriend. Running was the foundation that connected us. I had run over fifty races on Varsity through cross-country and indoor and outdoor track. He knew my running times, he saw my name in the newspaper, and there were Dad's words saying *the other girls in my races looked five inches taller,* the compliment was to cover what we both knew. He hadn't been there enough.

I saw him once. I was warming up for my race during an indoor track meet. I was sixteen. It was my junior year. I saw him when I ran by the entrance and orange doors at Manley Field house. He was standing under the stadium awning and I took another lap before meeting him.

The brim of his hat had created a slight shadow against his eyes. We both are surprised to see each other. The dry air of the indoor track arena met his cold jacket and after we hugged, I realized how unnatural it was. He looked older than his age, his untamed graying hair spurting out the sides of his hat, his eyes watery behind huge eyeglasses that slant off center, in need of repair, his eyebrows bushy, a mess, not rising with gusto like when he sang on the porch of the green house.

I was relieved he faded into the background of the arena, where it's dim by the exit doors. It might have been a bus, or a friend dropping him off at a corner outside of the arena, his face looked windblown and blotchy, from walking a distance in the cold.

I tried not to imagine where he lived, I didn't know. It had been a couple months since I saw him in person. Instead of looking directly at him I looked past his face to the side of his hat, speaking on the phone with some distance between us and able to jump from tangent and topic that had suited us but in front of me he was a stranger. Maybe he knew he wasn't that important while standing as a visitor in my zone. The high jump pit, the long jump, the shot put throwers grunting, cheers at the long jump, the gun going off for another race, enough noise between the silences in our conversation.

Since he got out of Jamesville Correctional Facility, I saw him in short visits at Mom's house, if someone else he knew could drop him off for an hour. We mostly spoke on the phone, and he would try to make it to my track meet this week, but he says that usually every week, if he could get a ride. I was doubtful, only there he was. I wished he wasn't.

I busted through an impending quietness between us. "—I already ran the 4/400, the last leg. We were behind but I got us up to third place. I beat my PR in the 400 too last week, my personal record." I reminded him, but he knew what I had meant, runner-talk.

"You're still the running rebel to me," he said. I let his compliment hug my heart for a tenth of a second, I hoped no one was looking at us and I wished he would leave. My stomach started to swirl; my nerves rattled more than usual before my races. A gun went off for another race behind us. The rhythm of feet churning up the six-lane running track behind me, the exhilaration, my place, and my shortcomings in my face.

Every time I do my best on the track, the last name we share is given a fresh slate. Even when it's not his voice calling my name down the last stretch. I inhaled the dry air. I wanted to go, finish warming up.

After he died, his health records would show he was failing to comply with his probation sentence of five years, there had been slip ups with the alcohol-sensor from his probation officer, it was positive. He was discharged unsuccessfully from an alcohol treatment program because of too many missed appointments. He had been arrested for aggravated harassment and was sentenced to Restored Probation after violating the original conditions of his probation sentence.

After being in the Jamesville Correctional Facility, he became a fungus, dragging on about problems. I didn't want to be the one thing keeping him hopeful but knew with running I was.

I could hear the cheers of parents and coaches loudly telling other runners to stay with it during their race. The other fathers who cheered for me too. Along with the 4/400 relay, I'm running the rare 500-meter dash next, I say. I have never raced the 500-meter race. My heart goes weak. I start to feel my competition warming up nearby, taking notice of the team's name on my uniform, the orange and white color, taking notice of Dad's crusty shoes and floppy shoelaces.

"I've got to go to get ready." My teammates are stretching down at our team's hub, I had to go. When he said I would do great, he had paid $5.00 just to get into the field house to watch me run. I smiled but he had missed so much. I had run my best races without him.

"I got to go warm up," I said, adjusting my running flats. He hadn't seen my shoe come off during the start of the 800-meter track race at Manley Field House, and I ran the whole thing with one shoe on. I triple knotted my laces now.

"I'll wave to you before the race." I told him.

"Here. For after your race." He said, handing me the plastic bag. I see an orange and an apple.   I gave him a quick hug goodbye. He reached for a cigarette in his inner coat pocket, as though he wouldn't be staying much longer after my race.

"I'll eat this on the bus back." I raise the plastic bag of fruit as I jet off to warm up.

A little later, when I jogged over to the starting line, I gave him a quick thumbs up, but once I'm in my lane I tried not to see him and his sullen eyes.

He is discreet, partly non-existent under the bright lights, where I show my best each week. Where I worked with determination and pushed harder until my heart exploded out of my chest. I continued to stretch my arms and look away from his difficult situation and lack of stability and car. I worked through every mile during training to not let the thought of his mistakes hold me back, and drain out my ability to strive, I worked to move forward when I hit the curves on this indoor track and then again with the burn in my chest right before I dry heaved and puked afterward to literally run my guts out.

There was the 4/400 at O.H.S.L North Division Championship, my relay team was First Place All League. I missed him being there then, but now felt maybe it was better he wasn't.

When I turned sixteen last fall, his birthday card read, *I'm very proud if you for more than just sixteen reasons.* He had added to *Always try to be kind and patient with everyone you meet and they most often will give you the same in return.*

I was trying to be patient with him.

My legs are jittery, my stomach swirling with nerves, but while I run I forget the worst facets of my life. At the starting line, the hours of training have made the possibility of accomplishment more than a pipedream. Desire and fear lead me while battling with another runner, each push of my legs and arms lead to the shine of a medal or soft silk of a ribbon in my hand. On the bus afterwards I would think about what lies beyond my hometown and leaving it all behind for something more.

I wrote inspirational notes to the team before each race: *It's the beat inside that lets you achieve, run with your heart.* Other times my writings went deeper, *you must never give in, fight from within, push with all yourself, feel the glory, feel the burn, feel the good in what you've done. A team is something that pushes you and stands by you no matter what. You may run feeling alone in the dirt shuffle, but the team runs with you no matter where you go.*

Running all year through the seasons and elements, the snow, sleet, rain, and the heat, had become constant solid ground, a normalcy to count on.

My father and I had spoken on the phone, and he knew I had been the co-captain of the cross-country team last fall, and he knew Coach suggested me for student of the month that October for the school newspaper, but my father didn't see me die on the trail each week, or know that while racing I'd yell "Come on!" breathlessly to my team-mates, and they would yell back and we were a unit, always together.

Every fall I'd pound over the hill at Long Branch Park at the northern end of Onondaga Lake, pumping my arms higher, and drudge myself over the top, not stopping. If I slow down at the top it's all over, hauling my legs over that hill, into the earth and holding onto my place in the pack for dear life, the air smelling of pine and chestnut trees. Dad wouldn't see me whip out of the woods breathlessly, but he was there when I got a scar above my eyebrow from the hill. I must have been nine or ten when my father took me and my sister sledding there and he left to move his car closer. I sledded down the wrong side of the hill, with roots under the snow and ice. I bled all over that hill. That hill is on my face.

Dad wore a wind breaker to a couple of my outdoor track meets at my high school. Outdoor track meant leggings and baby oil on my legs to keep them warm, long sleeves under my uniform jersey. Dad stood by the stands in front of the exchange zone on the track, and said he locked his bike at the crisscross metal fence while I was stretching with my teammates in the field. I didn't want to ask. I didn't want a teammate hearing him explain the trouble and effort it took to bike all the way here.

He took off his hat to wipe sweat off his forehead. His health records would later show he lived in an apartment complex with a friend. On the phone. I mentioned I had started practicing hurdling techniques, I knew he had run the high hurdles in high school too. I was mastering a swift leap, no stuttering feet to the hurdle, in rhythm with my steps, but he missed my winning race in the 400-meter hurdles that morning.

I was the last leg of the 4/400 next, one quick lap around the track.

I could see him eyeing his watch, and the brim of his hat tilted downward against the sunshine. While waiting for the baton pass, my arms waved frantically at my teammate, when she ran down the last straight away, I jumped around in my lane, yelling enthusiastically, "Come on, come on, come on, let's go. Let's go!"

When my arm swung back, the cold smooth metal in my hand was a cue to go full speed through the first curve. At the 200 meter long straight away, I felt strength in my legs pounding it down. Nothing could feel better. I would glide into the three-hundred-meter curve knowing it's where to give anything left. I plow down the last straight away. My legs throbbing during the final seconds of the race, because these lanes held the path for my future.

I qualified for the New York State Meet with the winning Section III Class A time in the 400 meters. I'd qualified for the Empire State Games held at Hofstra on Long Island, I ran at Junior Olympics in New Jersey that summer at Rutgers University. I felt on fire, my fastest 400-meter run was 60.9 seconds.

I had run eleven seasons in high school, and so much further than my hopeful lap around the dirt track. I had uprooted myself, become my truest self while running cross-country and indoor and outdoor track, never in socks and always in bright colored running flats, ribbons covered my bedroom wall and newspaper clippings were safely placed in my binders as proof I was good enough for an athletic scholarship. A scholarship to run track and cross country at a collegiate level was all I wished for, but if I didn't seek it, it wouldn't happen.

A community college nearby wouldn't cut it, my grades were not everything I told myself, I wanted to at least try to become a college athlete.

The phone and the mailbox were dead quiet. My best grades came from art and English class so I focused on finding a school with an Advertising major and running a program; my pathway to my dream.

Since sophomore year in high school, I had attended the cross-country Manhattan Invitational in Van Cortlandt Park. After the race I walked on Broadway with my teammates and we went to a musical. I aligned with the fluid movements around me, a rush of assertiveness on the cement that made me curious for what was beyond Times Square.

I flipped pages and dogged eared corners of a huge college directory book for options beyond Central New York. I contacted the coach from a college on Long Island and I shared my running times and achievements.

After being invited on a tour and visiting the campus and training facilities, it seemed to be the best and only option I had. I worked on my college application and first draft of my college essay about a moment in my life that made an impact on me and at first I wrote about my father and running.

...Running is a stress relief...when I run my determined spirit comes alive.

...Feeling power over my troubles and gives me a sense of control over anything bothering me."

...Just as my father inspired me to run, I inspire him not to drink.

Then I wrote another completely different essay about the qualifying race that sent me to the New York State meet. I wrote about the burn in my guts, ignoring the pain and my legs feeling like jello while fighting the other runner to prove how strong you really are.

When an envelope arrived I ripped it open. I wasn't going to be a girl from Liverpool forever, I had received a $10,000 athletic scholarship and would be running Division II—everything I wanted was in my hands.

In a photo from my high school graduation, I'm standing aside Dad with a wide smile, I'm holding my diploma, graduation cap and a bunch of white carnations he had brought me. Dad's graduation card read *May all your life's ambitions and graduation dreams come true.* I'd still have it, ten years later when my dad died and read his words again.

I was fleeing. The chance to be closer, to strike a bond more fully with my father would be gone.

My mom's car is full with college supplies we bought at Walmart, there would be a huge box at my feet and a humongous storage container attached to the roof of the car. Dad is still without a car and hates to arrange rides for himself, but he does to say goodbye. We stood in the driveway of Mom's house.

I'll call you, I tell him and hug him. I'm not sure I will too often.

I'm not sure if he will be staying at the home of the phone number he gave me too much longer anyways. I can't wait to be in the dorms on Long Island tomorrow.

I got the sense he will tell everyone he meets, *My daughter is down on Long Island... studying Advertising... on a scholarship...she'll be home for Thanksgiving.*

He handed me a few bucks and told me to buy a sandwich when I got there, to Long Island, over 300 miles away.

Thanksgiving seems forever away.

I needed a break from his mistakes and being his support-system.

I took his few bucks and he said in one of his Shakespearean voices, "And goodbye...for now, " I was unsure of when I would see him again.

Mom drove me down to Long Island. I didn't have my license to drive myself. The year before, on the way to Carousel Mall now called Destiny USA, I had been in a car accident with one of my friends on Onondaga parkway. I was put on a stretcher with a broken nose, and I was still too nervous to go for my driver's test.

On Long Island I don't think it will be a concern to not have a car, there are buses that go from the two campuses. Also, there's the

Long Island Railroad to explore the Manhattan campus on Columbus Circle—I was keeping that in mind.

After arriving at the Long Island campus with my athletic scholarship, I had new shoes, a new team uniform, and I achieved what I thought was everything I ever wanted, although the feeling wouldn't last.

Visiting the college campus and track had surpassed my expectations at the time, but the juice inside my legs wouldn't churn after a month there. I couldn't feel the spark at my heel or stamina while training with my new team, something in me had reached the peak, and a place of hunger inside of me that had been stirred up before practice had turned stale. I slumped, uncharged each time my legs tried to push further. I dragged through each drill and my flame wouldn't light. The beat I ran to, the victory song in my veins was a soft strum.

I had given running everything I had to give and it was over. By the end of the first semester at college I simply didn't need to run anymore. Dad, his lack of a car and license and my hometown were hours away and I didn't expect Mom to make every race. I had hit a wall, and I don't remember talking to my father about quitting.

I sent a letter to the college coach, knowing I would lose my scholarship that less than a year before I wanted so desperately, and now instead of asking for a chance I explained that I didn't have in my heart to run anymore.

While sitting next to father on the bench near the marina at Onondaga Lake, I looked at his worn Giants hat, I hadn't run as far as I might have gone but running had given my heart valuable lessons of the perseverance it took to give yourself a chance when the odds were against you, to keep courage and remain both patient and determined after a letdown, to create opportunity in each step. When I could have run off course every training mile and race navigated me toward something better, running had grown my aspirations and led me beyond these tree-lined streets of my hometown.

Maybe he knew running would be there for me more than himself. I wouldn't get to tell him how those old days at Zogg had made a difference in my life.

On the way back to the library we said goodbye. Standing there we took a photo side by side, my smile was big, my teeth jutting out into the awkwardness, I hadn't taken many photos with him. I looked at the camera, and he looked at me.

Death Day

How do you honor the anniversary of a death of a grandparent who will not meet his grandchildren? How do you honor such a terrible day in your life.

The sadness of unsaid words, what was missed, time not able to get back, this pain and longing, has been represented in gifts to my children.

I've bought my children space books, comic books and superhero figurines in memory of my father who liked reading comic books as a kid, something I learned after he died. We've gone through the photo album I made of photos of him, we've shared Snickers candy bars, *my dad's favorite*.

On the anniversary of his death, some years I've gone on long walks in nature. I've done nothing, busy with schedules and motherhood, the day would slip passed me and I'd get in bed and realize I did nothing.

I'd have a moment of silence while unloading the dishwasher and imagining my father walking away from me, turning and waving. Some years I've sent a donation to the SPCA in memory of his love of his pets and animal welfare.

Or I'd play one of his favorite songs and I'd watch an old movie he liked. I'd pause for a few minutes and read his letters or listen to couple of his voicemails thinking about how another year has gone by.

Silver Rings

At the funeral home I signed off on some end-of-life paperwork, and I could feel the weight of my father's urn in my lap. I hugged the wooden box with his ashes inside with one hand gripping the baggie from the coroner with his rings coated in soot. A vision of the barn came to me, the firemen searching for him, these rings right from dad's hand.

On the plane that evening back to Manhattan I studied the maze design of one of the bands, noticing the smut in the crevices, wondering how the roads of his life led to such a brutal way to die.

In lower Manhattan I walked over to a jewelry store with both rings. I asked for the silver band to be cleaned up, I would give it to my sister, then I asked that the engraved ring with the maze design not be cleaned deeply, only enough to get a little soot out of the crevices. I wanted to keep this maze-like ring in its natural form, not shiny, not glistening silver, but burnt. The engraved ring would help me feel closer to him, something that had been with him that morning, it would become my favorite object from his life.

I was glad my father's phone worked, other times he used a prepaid for calls, or would call from various friend's phones to leave me a message with a strange number to call him back on. I listen to him rant about life being hell, while the autumn sun hit my cheek. I sighed with him when he told me about being evicted from the house near my high school that he had managed to live in for a couple years.

In my other ear there was some chatter below from office workers on a lunch break, taxis honking and trucks, the brakes irk and stop while it makes deliveries in downtown Manhattan near Water Street. Then my father's complaints irk and ramble of days gone and misfortune, and a better life in the distance turned to dread.

My birthday had just passed, I was twenty-four, and sitting in a lounge chair on the deck at my boyfriend's apartment while he was at work, I was writing in my journal, at ease with the isolation and the gray buildings around me while plotting new goals, jotting down plans, debating if I should continue to pursue modeling or just start over my life with a realistic plan, when my father called.

An apartment of a friend, his car for a couple nights, and he mentions three nights in the homeless shelter, he starts laying out a timeline of all the places he has lived in the past month.

He says his ring has been stolen, it was taken when he took a shower at the shelter. A thick silver ring with a maze-design engraved on it. I always noticed the intricate design. Even though our relationship has become distant lately, even though I'm half listening now, I suddenly felt an urge to replace the maze ring.

Dad started talking about selfishness and scoundrels and how much he wanted some peace and quiet, he wanted to find some value in life again. He will stay with a friend, somewhere in Solvay outside of Syracuse, he said between rants.

"I could help people," he said.

"I could help people, like myself," he added, explaining that his depression was situational.

After my father died and years after this phone call, while looking at his health records I retrieved from the Syracuse VA Medical Center, the counselor notes show he was evicted from a home he was living in for several years, and I'd see the three days he spent at the Rescue Mission following an eviction. It reads that he was planning to apply for public assistance. In capital letters it reads he is homeless and unemployed.

Interestingly, in the records there's a questionnaire about his education. In his answers I learn for the first time the timeline of his college experience and his academic path in his own words.

He wrote that his focus in High School was science and when he attended Corning Community College and majored in Human Services. "I began college but enlisted into the Army from 1970-1972. Upon my discharge I returned to school," he wrote. He had graduated Corning Community College in 1973 with an associate degree, then he attended New York State College at Oswego and majored in Social Science.

Through my sleuthing for more information about his college years, I struck up a conversation with my mom about how she met my father and discovered they met at a bar in Oswego, maybe it was his wild reddish and curly hair that caught her eye. A photo in a family album shows his hair almost to his shoulders, a poofy curly-q mane. My mother had a teaching job in the Binghamton area while Dad finished up his degree at Binghamton University, she explained.

I will eventually dig for his diploma from Binghamton and after corresponding with the university I would receive his diploma and transcripts that show he was taking classes on Deviant Behavior and Cultural Relations, Racial and Cultural Relations. His health records explain that after he graduated from Binghamton, he had attended University College at Syracuse University, and was pursuing a Social Science Major, he took several graduate courses but did not complete the program.

"I should have continued my education," my father said on the phone. "I know a lot about psychology, I am well read. I know what my problems are," he gives me his spiel again about how drinking stole the better years of his life.

From reading his academic timeline, he clearly felt purpose in his studies and spent years mastering material on psychology or social work, but he never applied it to his life. He was he graduated from Binghamton, did he not find value in his studies, I wonder why he didn't have a developed plan for how to use these skills he gained.

I see during the time when his silver ring was stolen, he had been creating a new resume at a community center and wrote in the questionnaire he was "impaired because of my anxiety over lack of housing."

On the phone he reflected on going through a community care program that would help him find work. Although later, after he died, the records showed he violated some rules and wasn't allowed back in the program.

During the next couple of years, the progress notes explain he had a desire to obtain full time employment and his struggles to re-organize his priorities and focus on getting re-established. It reads he was limited in his capacity for work because of psycho-social circumstances and has a diagnosis of anxiety disorder, gout, and hypertension.

The notes explain his vocational handicap, his disability of an anxiety disorder caused a vocational handicap, and after vocational counseling and career exploration it states my father achieved his desired goals of employment working as a telemarketer, and working for home improvement sales, canvassing potential customers.

On the phone with him I didn't want to talk about resumes. I hadn't yet put to use my college degree in Advertising either, we have in common. Not using the certifications that we have, but I wanted to keep some distance between the things he hadn't accomplished and what I hadn't pursued. I wanted to stay motivated for my own in-progress pursuits and figure out the direction of my own life.

I had spent the past five years building my modeling portfolio—after quitting running I transferred to the Manhattan campus for my sophomore year, I lived in the dorms in Brooklyn Heights catching the 2 train up to Columbus Circle in the city for my Advertising courses, only I didn't want to create the ad campaign concepts in my classes, while looking in magazines I suddenly wanted to be in the advertisement. I wanted to reinvent myself.

I started growing it in-between my classes to meet with amatuer photographers I met through social networking websites and photography and modeling forums online. It was one crappy photo after crappy photo.

It was a pipedream. The photos I sent out to modeling agencies probably were thrown in the trash, my phone never rang but I was obsessed with updating my modeling portfolio that I bought at an art store, zipping to class, and back down to a test shoot with some amatuer photographer, hopeful this time wouldn't be another set of more photos that didn't have real potential for real modeling. I had to train my eyes to see what was marketable about myself beyond my lack of height.

I created a new name for myself, Isobella. I met a photographer who photographed television executives and soap opera actresses and worked with magazines, and surprisingly during the summer before my junior year of college, he knew the editor at a women's lifestyle magazine found at the check-out at every grocery store. I gained my first modeling tear sheet in the magazine. In the makeover editorial my eyes are the focus, my hair was trimmed, bangs cut above my eyebrows, and there was my gap teeth and overbite smiling back at me.

My face in a magazine.

I resubmitted my photos once again spending my food money on printing another modeling composite card showing my best photos and pursuing print modeling agencies that worked with models of all ages and types. I crossed my fingers and waited.

My foot had literally got me in the door with one print modeling agency who must have noticed my shoe size on my modeling comp card. Size six shoe. My feet had run hundreds of miles, they had been smashed in my running flats for years, but they still were in good shape. I started getting pedicures. I really didn't expect my foot and legs to be the force of getting a step into the modeling door.

I worked as a mannequin at a shoe store, I worked the spray tan booth at the Beauty Expo, and I had been one of the lead girls in a music video for a band that would later be on the cover of Rolling Stone magazine. I scrapped my credits together and some days it seemed as though I wasn't a fool.

Visiting the Syracuse area could mean missing an opportunity that could arise and Manhattan started to become my true home.

Finally, at the start of my senior year of college, one of the top body parts modeling agencies in New York City had called. She sent me to a handful of shoe modeling castings for high-end brands and show rooms for stilettos I could never afford to buy. I carefully watched while getting a pedicure, they had to be just right, yet after running to showroom after showroom, nothing fit perfectly enough.

There is a blank page, a distance between us while I was finishing college, I look at his health records to find a clue and don't see anything for those years. It makes sense though when I look ahead and see in the notes he was requesting a supply of gout medication and he hasn't been to the clinic for a couple of years.

When I graduated college, I gripped my modeling portfolio tight, eagerly skitter-scatting down the street in my mint-colored heels for the subway. Rent is due too quickly for my one-bedroom apartment in Queens, and modeling jobs are not coming in fast enough, it takes too long to get paid even though I booked another shoe modeling show. I wrote in my journal about this all being a waste and maybe I should go get a corporate job to pay my rent or maybe I just needed another chance make it through another month.

The door had opened, but it was getting harder to hold it open.

I lived on Wendy's dollar menu, fixed the scuffs on my shoes with a black marker before a go-see with an editor at a magazine, and wore out my welcome at the Apple Store in SoHo, using the display computers as my make-shift office to check emails, write, decompress and regroup my thoughts of wanting to toss my torn modeling portfolio in the trash on the days my email box was uninspiring, and the phone was too quiet.

I had booked a job with the Spanish network Univision, portraying the lead as a Latina even though I wasn't. I would do whatever it took. In hopes of paying rent consistently, I stood with these tall giraffe size models waiting to be chosen as one of hair models at the Wella Salon in Rockefeller Plaza, and would surrender my hair over and over again and let the stylists in training do whatever they wanted, making my hair shorter to pay rent. Now looking nothing like the photographs in my portfolio.

The thing keeping me hopeful was this one job I had booked with a well-known shaving brand, proving I could indeed be smaller than most models but still get opportunities with bigger brands. It didn't matter that my first advertising job with a world-renowned shaving brand would happen on a day I was cursed and had to borrow feminine supplies from the receptionist because it was my time of the month, or that the job involved my legs and lower body, because if I could live through that day there was no stopping me. Still, I had gone to appointments on 1st Avenue in Manhattan about becoming an egg donor. It paid a humongous amount if you qualified. I would've gladly given away some of my eggs, but when I answered questions about my family health, I accidently mentioned my father's alcohol addiction and his time in rehab, and I wasn't able to continue into the donor program.

I didn't tell my father about that, but I did tell him about my strain of the rent, and he had written me two short letters.

I hope this $8.00 helps a-little.

maybe you can buy a couple bananas

and some more pasta haha

Eggs are good too if you like them w alittle sausage etc.

I'll send you alittle more when I can.

If you take a P.R job it may prove more valuable as a modeling or design contacts and assn.?

I'm very proud to you

When I read the word eggs I was tempted to tell him about the egg donor letdown but instead we talked about me taking a job in public relations. I even went on the interview after our chat, but I didn't want the job. I didn't need a lunch break, and I was fine with twenty-five cent bananas from the fruit stand and hustling for the next opportunity in front of the camera. Dad told me how he was renting a house right on Wetzel Road, right near my high school. He liked living by himself, making omelets, reading the paper, and watching Turner Classic Movies. It was a better period for him until he got evicted, went to the Rescue Mission and lost his ring.

A week later he sent another short letter.

I hope you find less expensive accommodations, your going to make it Big Time I know this. Buy an apple and some oranges, maybe even instant potatoes and an onion or a little candy on sale, and maybe a couple of grapes, eggs are always easy & a piece of cheese for an omelet.

Only I just couldn't hack it anymore.

I begged my landlord to end the lease. I carried with me only what I could carry in a small suitcase and bounced from friend's couch to friend's couch, clinging to desperation for a few months. The bump of my suitcase over the sidewalk cracks was the sound of failure, but I wasn't going to give up modeling, I pulled my suitcase forward, heading for the subway to a friend's place in Hoboken.

Throughout the winter and spring as my amenities and bank balance got lower, I felt closer to my father suddenly. We would bounce our difficulties off each other, our financial woes, we had survival in common, the journey of life he spoke about being not easy.

We couldn't help each other get ahead but our conversations had become more than about his weakness point, it was mine too. While discussing my choices and wondering if I made a mistake my father would tell me about the medication he was on for his gout attacks, and the refills he needed, or the cigarette he was rolling. Sometimes we'd talk multiple times a day, and then weeks would pass. It all depended on the moment, how fragile it seemed, and if Dad had access to a phone.

As the summer started, I had finally rounded up enough modeling paychecks to feel a safety net, a cushion, and I had met my boyfriend and had basically moved in with him with my suitcase. Life seemed to stabilize for me, just when Dad mentioned losing his silver ring with the maze design, I listened to his tale of his issues being situational, and he spoke rapidly about the shelter being unsafe and how he wanted to one day return to the suburbs.

After he died, I'll discover in his health records that he was diagnosed with an anxiety disorder and hypertension around this time.

I was starting to get some publicity in city newspapers for my story about working in the modeling industry as a shorter than average model, modeling with my hands and feet for magazines and advertising campaign and writing essays about these experiences and accomplishments. I didn't want to think about my father's displacement. I wanted to end the conversation, when he said the felony he received for those DWI's years back was still right on his back during a background check. He's doing part-time under the table construction sales work, and when I tell him he could find other work in relation to his interest in helping people, he explains again that desperation makes him do desperate things.

I've got to go, I've got to run to the train to a meeting near Union Square, I wanted to say to him, he didn't know where that was, he never visited me in the city. I wanted to go about my self-editing, self-critiquing, waiting for my modeling agent to call, and take a breath away from his letdowns in life. I'm tensed up from my own shadow of instability, the weight of a pendulum taking deep plunges between the fast-pace momentum of possibility in my day that I wanted to keep alive, and the slow drag of regret that is his.

I didn't want to listen when he told me about having lunch some days at a community center, sometimes he does his laundry there and he can always call me from there he confirmed. I listen though, for a few minutes longer—for the sake that he had listened to me when I had felt uncertain about my next moves during the year before this phone call.

On the phone with him then, my chest felt tense when he spoke about grabbing lunch at the Rescue Mission. I imagined him lying on a cot at the shelter for a few nights, his thinning hair, his deep sigh as he settled to sleep, wearing the same clothes again, his eyes closing, his belongings beside him. Maybe under his cot was a tattered World Almanac he's brought with him, maybe his glasses were folded in his hands peacefully, while falling asleep there, and he's quiet and contemplating his options for tomorrow, and life beyond this dimension in time.

I pictured his face, older now, his bushy eyebrows narrowing when he said something about being older now.

"Please surround yourself with positive people, things will get better," I said in a hurry.

I wanted to know his ring size before we hung up.

A part of me greatly wanted to live in the moment, be with my boyfriend, make some dinner plans and walk to the Seaport for French onion soup, and not think about my father's burdens, but I grabbed my purse and started walking to the train.

A new ring will be a reminder of hope, and it will be shiny, I told myself. I swiped my Metro card. I needed to find one with a similar maze design, the design itself will somehow keep him on the path to a better life, keep his face toward the sun, no matter the uncertainty of tomorrow and his lack of a home address.

I went a couple stops on the uptown train to SoHo, near the Apple store. I knew the area always had street vendors near Prince Street and Broadway. I hadn't bought my father much of anything in recent years besides a flannel at his birthday in mid-February. I dashed up the subway stairs at Prince Street while promising to myself to visit Syracuse soon, to call my father back more often, to listen to his voicemails and hear his every word. I planned out a letter I'd write him with some positive anecdotes, as I walk on Broadway quickly with the shuffle of foot-traffic around me.

I scanned the rings at a jewelry vendor street stand, searching for one just right, a ring with carved paths that wrap all the way around the band. I went to another jewelry stand and another. Until I spot one ring with a design that stood out, it was close enough.

I buy a plain silver band as well, since the street stand sale says there's a discounted price for buying two rings. By looking at these rings maybe he could believe that lunch at the Rescue Mission wasn't going to be forever. His missteps and the years of his life now gone, didn't define his existence or worth, he could plow through the letdowns and dead-ends, because the clock hadn't run out, there time left for a restart. There was uncertainty of when I would hear from him again as I got on the train, but these rings in my pocket would represent some hope for better days.

I'd give him the rings the next time I visited Syracuse that fall—and a few years later he'd have them on the morning when he died in the fire at his home, when the sheriff asked if my father wore any jewelry.

THE NIGHT I LOST MY FALLOPIAN TUBE

The sonogram showed the fetus was in my fallopian tube-and I had to have surgery immediately. What I thought was a miscarriage was now an ectopic pregnancy. The doctor said I needed to have the surgery today as soon as I could get there.

I couldn't reach my spouse at work, my son was with a babysitter, my phone dying as I called my mom in a cab. I had passed the word ectopic in pregnancy books while carrying Phoenix but never imagined "that" happening to me but now I was that statistic, out of the blue. A fetus in the fallopian tube can kill you. I checked myself into the hospital where my son was born. I signed my name on paperwork about the procedure. I sit alone waiting to be called.

This is when I begin to understand the loneness of not having immediately relatives nearby and I joke to the nurses about needing a nap before the anesthesia.

My son wakes me up jumping on my hospital bed and we embrace, my one and only, sweet boy.

There was a heart bandage on my belly button where the incision was made. I lost a tube, and I spent only a brief time in that place of dark wonder and whys, but then focused on trying again. After losing my father in a fire, this pregnancy loss, this grief somehow is incomparable, the vein that connects bloodlines knows I've felt worse. I wanted to move on quickly.

Somehow, I'm 8 weeks and 3 days, I can hardly believe it. A baby before Christmas! We will see, hoping it is in good spot this time to bring me another bundle, a glow, a girl.

When she is born, we both have a small dot, a birthmark on our palms.

Voicemails

He passed away peacefully at home surrounded by his family—Nope. I often think about the ice splitting the gas line. Then I will think about the last time I spoke to him, and I'll turn to these messages, these last words from him. In the messages he is here, moving throughout his day, the day is new, the day is long and then his time on earth is, I know, gone. To have this sudden disconnect, the line dead between us, words unsaid burrowed in my chest, means a part of me remains in the doorway of that phone call from the sheriff.

The messages were lost. The week before I had a new cell phone, so I only had one voicemail from my father on it. That message was from Friday. The fire happened the next morning. After the call with the sheriff, I had an urgency to get my father's voicemails back.

I knew he had left me a ton of messages on my old phone. He was on my phone plan, so I would have access to his phone records, and I had the ability to get mobile carrier to put the voicemails back on my new phone somehow. It was a miracle.

Listening to these messages became essential and a comfort. Maybe because talking in person was talking on the phone. I created a new routine in my day, brew coffee and press play, pace the apartment listening to him breathing, coughing, asking me to call him back, and then walk, pressing my ear to the sound of his voice, every um, while walking through the city. The sirens and honks of taxis rushing by, I heard none of it, walking slow, I followed the trail of his tangents, talking in real-time faded away, and replayed his voice again.

Don't go, don't go. I'm tainted by the fragility of the earth turning into a new day, I know that tomorrow isn't a promise only a hope because I have his last message.

Having these voicemails back on my phone wasn't enough, because over time voicemails do disappear, or I fear.

Outside the Hudson River is sparkling with ice. Inside some gentle sunlight was coming through the closed blinds, and I settled on the bed. I liked the room dark, dim, the gray shadows while I caved up around my phone and a digital voice recorder, listening carefully as my father's speaks.

I bought one of those Olympus digital voice recorders, rectangular, thin, and white, with a USB that flipped out, at technology store, right by the Brooklyn Bridge. I played the voicemails on speakerphone and record each one individually and then upload them on my computer. I wrote down bits of each voicemail in my journal to remember which was from which date. Then I decided to transcribe each of them, word by word, and the ums, pauses and sighs.

Nineteen messages aren't as much as it seems, I can listen to the whole reel in just a few minutes then he is gone. But when I do listen, I'm in his day again, during that span the last two and half months of his life from early December through the end of February archived with his words.

I didn't listen to these messages, in the same way, when he was alive. I skimmed over them quickly while on the way to meet friends at a rooftop bar with heat lamps near the Flatiron building in Manhattan. Some voicemails from my father I barely listened to at all. I had even rolled my eyes at another message.

I hear my father saying, *I went to listen to your voicemail, but I pushed the other button, anyway, you can call me when you can.*

He forgot to click end on his phone. He doesn't know the voice-mail is still running. He's breathing heavy into the icy February air, huffing, and hacking up phlegm. He sounds older than he was. I hear movement, as if he's collecting some items before leaving his car. He sounds terrible coughing again. I wish I visited him more; my immediate thought is, he is alone. I want to walk with him, while he puts his hand up to block the freezing wind.

In another message he says, *I'm over here at the Nice and Easy gas station, I've been spending half my life in this place. They ought to have a rec center or something some kind of community place (cough) where people can go and not spend money*—I know where it is. The last time I saw him, over Thanksgiving, it was about three months before he died, I met him at the gas station with a convenience store, it's sort of run-down, he seemed to be a regular there.

In early February his message explains how to find meaning in life.

I got your message, you're on your way to Hell's Kitchen, well some people think hell is on earth and I'm beginning to believe that more as time goes by, couldn't be too much worse... in hell...

Then he swears and tells me about driving in the snow.

Okay, I'm pretty tired, I was out shoveling this morning. I, ah, had my tired rotated and they kept saying, oh well it won't do any good. Well, I knew fucking well, excuse me; I knew damn well, it would do good. Because the rear tires had traction and I don't care about the rear tires because I don't fish tail and I don't drive that fast and if I do fishtail, I know how to get out of it quick. So to make a long story short, I can get through the snow a lot easier and it cost $18 bucks, but it was worth it. They wanted to try to charge me 180 dollars for two front tires, ah that's ridiculous; I can get used ones for 10-15 dollars. I don't know why I'm talking about it, but I'm a little tired, but you'll have fun, see life is about fun if you don't hurt others.

Then he explains more about helping others.

But then you have to at some point, ah try to help others. Like you help me or you help somebody else. And, then your life is worth it. If you just sit around and do nothing all day and you don't volunteer to help anyone, then your life becomes useless and meaningless, and I see too much of that. Cause there's such a need, there's such a need that a healthy person, ah whose got a halfway decent mind, ah should be able, --but then they don't have conscious, they figured they've worked long enough and now they're going to do literally nothing. And I find it, I find it rather, ah, not only sad, but it angers me. When a healthy people—because there's a lot of elderly people, people, ya know 85-90 years old who help other people the same age, ya know they push em on a wheelchair, or they, they drive meals on wheels. And then you've got people that do nothing, they don't even help ah, ah animals or people. And they—that kind of a person disgusts me. I have no problem with a person who is ill themselves, mentally or physically because then they need help, but to just lie there and do nothing when you can do something, it just, well it disgusts me.

This voicemail truly captures the type of voicemails I never fully listened too at the time but now listen to over again. His words make me question the time I have spent, the time I have given. I can't help but close my eyes because he doesn't know he will die in a few weeks.

I see his kooky expressions when he says, *ah (laugh) watching this old movie with Mickey Rooney and some other people, Sally Forste and different ones...some of these were well known songs in the early 50s. I'll um talk to you later.*

But he didn't say goodbye. He kept talking.

That's a big win for Syracuse, because they can get recruiting from ah Long Island and ah New York and all these other ah East Coast Cities now, so it's very important to 'em.

He went on about the football game and then he thanked me for listening.

.... Anyways you don't need all these details but ah love you ah thanks a lot for everything. I just need somebody to ah be a sounding board for me. Sometimes you need just talk things over and ah... convince yourself what you're doing is right or wrong...

In a message that took place a month and a half before his death. It's one of my favorites because I hear his honesty comes through and true self in the pauses between his words. It's about his drinking.

I got your ah voicemail, ah not your voicemail your text message and your picture, ah pic is picture of course. So, if you want to talk in person, you can call me back. I have some time. See as long as you call before nine, usually I start falling asleep around nine, I might wake up uh again at ten and ah, it's just I've totally changed; I'm not the same person I was 10-15 years ago. Uh, I'm a farmer. I go to bed early. I get up real early, 3:30-4 o'clock in the morning. And ah in a way it's good because I have more energy in the mornings now. I used to have no energy in the mornings, course I'd be hung over a lot. I drank a lot, I drank more than some and less than others but definitely too much for too long. Okay, I'll expect your call, and ah if you don't want to call you can leave me another text message. I like this phone because I can do a lot more with it than I could with the other one. Okay, love you byebye.

It's as though he's asking for forgiveness, his words meet my complicated grief. The newspaper reporting the fire was at 6:10 am, and I can't help but wonder if he was awake when the fire broke and enflamed his home. I never told him I had valued our phone calls and relationship, I never got to say his words had meant something to me. I didn't know my father was going to die suddenly before dawn on a normal Saturday. I thought there'd be more words between us.

I find myself using his jargon in my daily conversations.

I'm out here in the driveway I was shoveling...

I can practically see his winter coat and the shovel he is using to clear the snow, the cigarette hanging out of his mouth while he does.

When he says, *anyway ah, I'm looking forward to getting your literature (a Shakespeare-ish accent) and I will give you some constructive criticism, nothing negative, all positive, on that, because sometimes you're too close to it,* he'd be gone next month.

Then, *Well I didn't hear a beep so I'm just going to start talking...Ah, well, I hope your writings going well, gimme me a call when you feel like talking, otherwise leave me a text message. One good thing about text message is you don't have to call. I mean you don't have to talk for 10-20 minutes.*

The voicemails vary from seconds up toward three minutes. As the years go by, sometimes I listen to them from furthest away to most recent— sometimes I listen to only his last one. Sometimes listen to a few and skip over others to get to my favorite ones or fast forward to a part that makes me smile and visualize his expression while he speaks. Sometimes we laugh together while I listen and I sigh with his tired voice while he's moving about his day, he's talking about what he is planning for tomorrow. He's alive, I can trick my mind for a moment to believe he just left this message for me that same day, in the quiet after listening to him speak, my grief can subside, but of course reality rushes in, the alarm to get my kids off the school bus blares, time has moved on without him.

Then everything I haven't accomplished meets him saying, *I'm very proud of your perseverance, it's not an easy journey, and nobody ever said it was...Things will get better for all of us... I'm confident of that.*

Maybe the future had been on his mind.

...Well thank you, I got the card and the... forty dollars, I'll ah, put it towards my car insurance. And it was very welcome. Um, call me anytime, I did send you a Valentine's Day greeting. (sniffle) I'm a little tired. Um, yeah, we still have snow out here, a lot of snow, but it's melting, and it will melt towards the end of the week, okay I love you and thank you again... bye for now.

It was a card for his birthday on February 12th, he would die in less than two weeks.

In another voicemail he says, *I really like being by myself. Mentally healthy you know. If you can stand being by yourself, you don't need to be around people.*

In my father's last voicemail to me, I've memorized the pauses in this one, the way his voice shifts high or low into another sentence, as though his words look me straight in the eye. *...Remember, absence*

*makes the grow heart fonder, and familiarity breeds contempt and... out
of sight out of mind...Anyways we got ourselves another blizzard. And ah,
we'll talk soon...*

I wish I could tell him about his grandchildren, how my son has some
freckles on his nose too, and an eyebrow that arches just the same. I tell
my kids; this is what your grandfather sounds like, and I play one or two
of his messages to give his words a pulse.

I see his eyebrow arch, his two-pocket flannel shirt, his Giant hat,
when he says, *We'll talk soon,* I let that echo in my mind, even though I
know we won't.

Moving Forward Walks

I think sudden loss is a lifelong healing process. A practice of observing grief emotions that are carried, how these emotions can change the person. After my father died I breathe differently, speak with less intensity, I'm calmer, in less of a rush, my father's death changed the way I walk. I found a place of solace at the arboretum in Houston, I've dropped a lot of grief there.

A gift of a rabbit dashing across the path, or a water snake holding its head above the pond water, on these walks, I would allow the bend in the long-stemmed flowers to meet my bowing head, their decaying stems, but somehow, they still reached for the sun, as though they knew there was another season to see. I make peace with my grief, the sound of my feet, the churn of my movements against the wood and dirt paths, a reminder that I am not broken. I see my favorite tall dead tree in the meadow. It once was full, vibrant and green, and is now branchless, a beam in an open space, a new home. It stands how I would like to be, strong and planted, mended, whole, ready to take on what may hurt. In this natural setting, my legs are in no hurry, I've shown up to the calm pond water, the pair of red cardinals that split in mid-air, a leap of a frog as I pass the boardwalk, the splash as if just for me, cheering me on, it will be better, while I'm moving steadily.

Answers

When my son was around 3 years old he asked me if I had a dad. I was surprised by his question and simply said, "He passed away before you were born." And then I added, "He is always in our hearts." I didn't exactly want to scare my son by saying his grandfather died in a terrible fire, and I didn't tell him about the pain from not getting to say goodbye, but that day I introduced the emotion of loss to my child. I'm sure he could see it on my face, but I didn't want to tell him that his grandfather was unidentifiable when he died, and the medical examiner said smut was in his lungs.

I would look at Phoenix's arched eyebrow — so much like my father's —and think of the green house, of running, of my father singing a tune. As my kids get older the questions occur more often, some harder to answer than others, how old was your father, how old would he be now? Did he have brothers and sisters? What did he do as his job, what was his favorite food?

CLIPBOARD

Handwriting is not only the words. It's the moment, where they were when they wrote it, the very imagining of their living mind, breathing self, full of thought, moving pen on the page. It's a brief moment in time, as if we were talking face to face. His pen had touched the card, his hands held it steady as he wrote, his fingers placed the card into the envelope.

Under more papers in the backseat of Dad's car his handwriting on a clipboard caught my attention. I was weeding through the random envelopes, receipts, and coffee cups thrown about in his car but stopped to study his written word on the back of a flyer for a moment. The capital letters mixed with cursive, the arrows and circles and underlines, a big coffee stain at the bottom corner of the front flyer seeped through all of the rest.

This supplement of his daily life. A brief record. A view of his day. A to-do list in the form of calls he made, follow ups needed, numbers and names. I follow this trail of where he's been when I read his notes, and

I can almost see him moving throughout his day in my hometown on the streets and roads of my childhood.

I imagine him going door to door or storefront to storefront. He's trying to deliver a sales lead for the home improvement company he's working with, every time his pen hits the paper, he's giving the day something new—even if he doesn't know if it will lead to anything, he's moving, going somewhere.

His persistence to keep going stays on my mind while I hold the clipboard, I will keep it. I imagine him crossing out the words that hung in the air when he said to me years ago that he didn't want to live.

I can hear his voice saying *Life's a Bitch And Then You Die* but not today.

His outlook that tomorrow could be better was here, I see it in the capitals, I study the fluid motion of his cursive. His pen that he was holding against these papers on the clipboard, there was more to jot down.

The sun beams off the Hudson River and through the window in my city apartment, I try out my father's clipboard in front of the bathroom mirror, holding it like he may have done.

I feel the rectangular shape around my fingers, the worn edges, maybe he would have held it under his arm aside his coat and ribs, before soliciting a flyer about roofing repairs or windows.

The clipboard with soft corners from wear, this hand-held accessory that had obviously been tossed in his car, grabbed and overworked but it lasted, as a good thing never dies.

The word Longbranch, is written in small capital letters. The big hill at Longbrach Park in middle school and high school cross-country meets. I wonder why he wrote it down, what he meant by writing the name of the street I lived on after my parents divorced, a few blocks from the green house. Maybe he was knocking on doors over there handing out flyers recently. There's even a fire department on his sales list. I trace my finger over the loops and straight lines of each letter, number and word. I unclip his business card attached to the clipboard.

These scraps of his life, these words he rushed to write, is now ink left behind.

The last time I saw him at his home, I didn't know that visit would be the last time I'd see him, when he ripped out of a small notebook a few pages of his writings. These words are not directed to me or anyone. It's his mind running. When life was a rolling treadmill of uncertainty and instability, and five loud roommates in the half-way house, written before he had moved to the rural landscape of Phoenix, New York, where he died.

Thoughts about statements

Soul & Kindness
Spirit & Meditation
Marks & Measures
Meaning & Wisdom
Purpose & Progress
Heart & Loving
Expression & Listening
Relief & Rejuvenation
Peace & Giving
Serenity & Well Being
Gratitude & Attitude

As it is offensive to be overly defensive, it is repugnant to be overly, coyly reluctant

I read these thoughts of my father and try to get inside his mind.

...Personal insecurity and quiet nature can often be misinterpreted as arrogance and egotism

...The tragedy of human existence now and in the past history is that violence, war and murder still is and always was an acceptable solution, to human problems, that always had their resolution in peaceful communications.

...If only 1/10th of 1% of the effort to achieve winning war was spent on negotiations for peace. War would and could not exist.

When the funeral director handed me Dad's veteran flag, I said I didn't want it. My father didn't need the flag I insisted, but the funeral director encouraged me to take it. He explained that regardless of whether my dad liked his time in the military, the United States still wanted to thank him for his service. So, I took the flag.

...The insidious technical assault on civilizations simple and more complex, is purposeless, mindless and without a goal other than to perpetuate itself and all of us into an ultimate soulless oblivion

...Superfluous Technology can not replace humanity. It can only dehumanize us. Ex. Nuclear bombs, rays, will ultimately destroy us all without selectivity or mercy. We can conceive of nothingness but cannot experience it. I dread tomorrow and envy the dead, a prisoner of sorrow, no peace in my head. Genius is often mistaken for foolishness or idiocy, but only so mistaken by fools and idiots.

Dad added a dash underline and writes below a description of actor Terrance Stephen McQueen and that *he played a heroic-anti hero, a gre-*

garious loner, and an exuberant introvert. He notes this was described by Ephraim Katz in the Film Encyclopedia.

I wonder if my father thought of himself as a *loner* and *exuberant introvert.*

I order myself a copy of the book.

Dad wrote down a quote from Ralph Waldo Emerson, *"A foolish consistency is the hobgoblin of little minds..."*

Then he added with a downward arrow, as is *"organization" to or without flexibility or elasticity.*

On the same notebook page, *Living without Interfering, Helping. Bragging, or Reminding or Belittling. Nobility is rooted in humility.*

Around the time he wrote these thoughts down, I had asked my father to join the phone plan my boyfriend and I shared.

I wanted to have a way to always know where my dad was and how he was doing.

Because his phone had been disconnected at the time, I had sent him a small package and letter with the news. He had previously told me to send any mail to him at the address of a contractor company he worked with doing sales work. It was safer that way, he said, than sending mail where he lived now. He called the place with the lunatics an asylum, where it could get misplaced among his roommates.

Dad and I had gone back and forth through letters and cards discussing a phone and he had written me back on lined paper:

I received your package and it was most welcome. Paul Newman article was well written and quite detailed. He got at least 3 roles James Dean had agreed to do before his tragic death. Thank you again, my phone is out of service, I'll get it back on or get another type of service maybe a track-phone number.

Dad had written back on the same card I had sent him hoping he was hanging in there and asking him to let me know how he was doing.

...Thank you for the letters of encouragement, tell me more about your cell phone idea. Perhaps I could see you soon, maybe I could borrow a car for a couple of hours; we could go to the lake again.

My pen ink is red, and my handwriting is large on the card.

Hi Dad,

I hope to find you okay. Enjoy this signed book by Alonzo Mourning. When it comes to the phone, basically if you wouldn't mind having a Texas number we can put you on the plan...

I explained his number would change and I wasn't sure that was good for him.

I should have known that changing his number wasn't an inconvenience. Any working phone would've done the job. I could tell in his card back to me that thinking about having one again made him feel a reboot.

Thank you so much for the autographed Zo (nickname) book. It is an inspirational account of a triumphant life. The $25.00 helped me a lot. And the stamps of course. Your suggestion of the cell phone would be much appreciated at this difficult time in my life. I do believe I have something good to contribute still in the future. We live in a world of uncertainty, but you have kept me (not to give up) hopeful.

...If it's true that "in the land of the blind the one-eyed man is king" then that man should use his limited vision to help those who cannot see at all; to maybe make this world a better place.

Eventually I got a new phone so I could give him my old one and put him on my phone plan.

A year later a card he sent me read.

...I'm still looking for a cheap but New York State inspectable vehicle, car, van, truck or SUV, Older for a few hundred dollars. I always enjoy speaking with you. The phone (call) means a lot to me. When I get a vehicle and a better job, I'll have a lot better attitude.

...Time is often our enemy, but the future can't be much worse.

...We need thoughtful and creative minds to counter the senseless ones who are unthinking and uncreative.

...I plan to write articles and commentaries about life as we know it and what alternatives to the status Quo we might employ.

There was a coupon for a cup of coffee in his letter.

After he died, I saw my own handwriting at his car, they were on a few envelopes that have been torn open. I sit with them now. The light blue card that I had sent him had been damp with water stains on the envelope—It was dated for Father's Day, a year before he died.

Dear Dad,

I love you, Happy Father's Day

Each day grow and try

Sometimes I laugh with the memory

I remember the time he told me on the phone how he plunged the toilet at a coffee shop. I think of this now and crack a smile. At the coffee shop the toilet was clogged and he spoke to the manager about it. The clog had been there for a while Dad told me on the phone.

"I fixed the toilet and took action and used the plunger obviously. It's not rocket science," he said.

Then he mocks the situation, "send it to the committee, it's a major corporate decision."

He was glad to help fix this small issue, he said.

He had explained his technique of lifting and pulling the plunger.

"You have to lift and pull; you have to LIFT! LIFT!"

I imagine Dad making a lifting motion with a plunger and saying, "...You can't just expect it to do it itself."

He seemed pleased about his good deed and said he got a free coffee afterward.

THERMOS

Drinking coffee warms up the hollowness, where the truth sits, where knowing that my father is alive, is gone. Next to his urn on coffee table is an envelope post-marketed for March 31; a little over a month after he died. I had requested the autopsy results. I had wanted the words, information, I wanted to read the narrative and visual description of what my dad looked like in the end.

A week before, on March 23, the subject of an email from my modeling agent said: Train for tomorrow. I read the details about the photo shoot in Hawthorne, New Jersey. I was to take the New Jersey Transit to the Glen Rock Main Line Station, and call the studio when I arrived, someone would pick me up. I was to be French pedicure-ready to have my feet photographed for a health care catalogue. My emails show I had written to my modeling agent, "I am 100% available anytime," and included a smiley face, only a week after my dad died. I didn't expect any photo shoots and bookings, I felt distracted from *life before death*, I didn't expect a job to appear. I could have said no. Maybe I needed to get out of the apartment, maybe I needed to be active and dig up some hopefulness and courage to put on a clean outfit, some lip gloss and look alive.

At Penn Station in Manhattan, I held the stainless-steel coffee thermos I found in my father's car. I imagined him drinking from it when I saw it in the cup holder, the coffee inside frozen solid. The silver stainless steel tumbler was something he probably used every day. I imagined him takin a sip from it while driving to his sales job, stopping at the local gas station down the road to fill it up and the coffee pepping him up for his day. *He breathed into this thermos.*

I brought the thermos along for luck. The warmth from the coffee I made this morning calms me. Even though I've washed the thermos and scrubbed at the inner sides of it with a sponge, it still smells like it did when I found it, cigarettes, and day-old coffee—the essence of Dad.

I thought about how Dad would talk fast, hyper from the caffeine. He liked to remind me that he was completely sober, and coffee had become his drink of choice. We both were coffee addicts.

I boarded the train bound for Hawthorne, New Jersey. Sitting at a window seat, I had my modeling portfolio in my bag next to me, and a tight grip on the thermos as the train lurched forward. This would be the day I almost lost this keepsake.

The call from the sheriff repeated each day. I couldn't shake the thought of large pieces of charred metal or wood being moved by firemen, and Dad underneath, his face being unidentifiable and the smell of ash in the air from the fire.

The rhythm of the train reminded me of my past trips to Syracuse before Dad moved to the country, when he didn't want me to visit him where he lived with his roommates. Instead, we'd sit across from each other at a small green table in the train station before my return trip back to Manhattan. I'd have all my luggage at my feet, I'd be wearing my favorite denim jacket and stilettos, maybe a silk bandana around my head. He'd wear a dress shirt with two pockets with an assortment of pens bursting out, and pants he'd pair with sneakers. His eyebrows rising behind his large eyeglasses while we caught up on each other's lives over train-station coffee.

During these visits I'd realize I wasn't embarrassed of him anymore, by his love of old broken thing he said were still good, his smokey smell, his DWI's, the felony, it seemed to matter less and instead I was sitting with this aging man, my dad.

I caught him up on my modeling career. Telling him even though I had finally booked a modeling job advertising shoes, and did photo-shoot in Central Park on the steps near the Bethesda Fountain and that I was hand modeling with a food magazine, the other castings weren't leading to much.

Whenever we said our goodbyes at the station, I'd tell him I'd call when I got back to the city. Sometimes I did. Sometimes a few weeks could pass before I thought to call him. I remembered hearing the Maple Line going to Manhattan being called; while I walked up the long ramp to the train platform, I didn't know I'd see my dad only a few more times. I had taken our train station visits, coffee-chats, phone calls, and our relationship for granted.

I don't know the direction I'm going or what is next, but I hear my arrival in Hawthorne, New Jersey, on the train announcement. I run my hands through my hair and try to forget about the fire for a minute and that this happened to my father.

All the time I've spent building my portfolio seems like a waste of time. Modeling in this moment seems superficial, just shallow. It's just my foot, it's just a shoe. All I had worked for, growing my modeling portfolio with magazine tear-sheets and experience, it doesn't seem as though it's been time well spent. The train was already pulling into the station in Hawthorne, though. I was expected to follow through, I traveled all this way, I was direct booked for this photo shoot; no casting this time; just photos shown from my agent to the marketing director. I wanted to honor my commitment to the job and who I'm expected to be.

I tried to focus on how I used to be, as I stood up. I will enter the photo studio with a friendly smile, I told myself. I'll be courteous and thankful for the lunch buffet, and plenty of coffee to refill up on. When the doors to the train opened, I tucked Dad's thermos into the side pocket of my bag.

I thought of my father's voicemail, him saying, *"I just need somebody to be a sounding board for me. Sometimes you need just talk things over and ah... convince yourself what you're doing is right or wrong."*

The photo studio is large and open like a warehouse and with high ceilings and multiple production sets in motion, with busy and creative energy. The art director welcomes me with a relaxed set of pants and a button-up shirt to change into. I swept my long hair up into a ponytail to keep it out of the shot. I placed my feet into soft warm slippers and stretchy foam flats and more comfort shoes. With each shoe, I delicately pointed my toe toward the camera and became unmoved, as though my whole body is meant to be still.

Holding a pose, putting pressure on my calves to hold a position, an orchestrated balance of breathing, precision, and staying quiet during the shot. I think about how my father liked the quiet, embraced silence, and had told me, it's mentally healthy to be ok being alone.

I focus on the task calmly with my limbs, legs and foot, frozen, exhaling softly to keep the right angle, while a photo assistant adjusts a strap on my shoe, or the photographer directs me to move my foot an inch this way or that.

The production crew took a short break, I filled up dad's thermos halfway, I added lotion to my legs and feet and changed into a new outfit before the next take, I try to forget about the pressure to be what is expected.

Back on set under the lights I worked hard to stay complacent, content, and dry-eyed. I focused deeply on the shoe, the color, the shape of it, the laces tied into a neat bow, remaining poised and professional, I was striving to get the image just right. I tried not to think about the last time I had used my feet to model it was for a magazine editorial on how to create your own nail polish designs, and Dad was alive.

With my eyes staring at my foot until it became blurry, I blinked at the sound of the camera's shutter, standing in a numb state. The photographer, assistants and art director were staring at me, at my foot, and I wanted to run back to the city, to my bed.

In my mind, I hear my dad's voice say, *"It's a not an easy journey, and nobody ever said it was."*

I told myself I was okay, I had been doing this type of work for years, but all I see are the words of the news stories, and photos of his home after it was engulfed with flames. The autopsy results would conclude Dad died of thermal injuries and inhalation of smoke from the fire and explosion. There was soot in his airways, throat, and nose. Full charring on his whole body except the areas of the neck and upper chest, to the bone in some areas of the lower legs, blackened to the ankles.

Only I don't know these full details yet. I just have my imagination to create a vision of what my dad looked like when he died. I don't have the autopsy description yet just the gutted structure in mind. I felt trapped inside the shoe I was wearing; time started to feel slower with each new style and while waiting for the photographer to adjust the lightning. The set suddenly felt too hot. I shouldn't have gotten out.

I think of dad's voicemail saying, *"I'm a little tired right now, had a long week, but things will get better for all of us, I'm confident of that."*

I hug everyone goodbye casually when the last shot is accomplished and eagerly grab my bag. I feel relief when I sit assistant's car to be taken back to the train station. It is over.

On the platform I wait for the Manhattan-bound train, pleased that I made it through the photoshoot without bawling or telling anyone what was really on my mind. I reached for my dad's thermos in the side pocket of my bag to savor the few last sips left. It wasn't there.

I dug around inside my bag furiously looking for it while the wind hit my cheek, my eyes were burning with tears. I couldn't find it.

I frantically called the studio phone number, blurting out to the first person who picked up, "I've lost my thermos," and asked if anyone can find it. My voice was choked up, as I spoke about the old thermos and the silver color.

I paced the platform: my eyes tearing up, heart racing, waiting, stuck there, hoping the thermos wasn't buried in the dark, somewhere way back behind a piece of furniture or photo studio supplies and unable to be seen under shoe boxes.

That moment of despair has stayed with me, years have gone by, and I still feel incredibly grateful for the assistant who drove back to the train station to bring me the found thermos. I had grabbed it, no longer the prim shoe model wearing a comfortable foamy shoe. I was carrying the debris and wreckage, the burnt metal from the fire on my back, the raging heat from the blast and the blistered ruins meeting the cold air, standing in a fog of lost time meeting the freezing wind against the pole-barn in the country when I clutched the thermos close to me.

I won't use it again, I tell myself. The thermos is too close to the day before my dad had died, it had already seen its last sips. On the way back to Manhattan, I closed my eyes and listened to the loud pulse of the train, the rocking sound held my irresponsibility, my foolishness as the keeper of what was left behind.

WHAT'S LEFT BEHIND

Years later I'd show my son and daughter a gray sweater and a World Almanac that never make it to my father. I hadn't made it to the post office and was late with sending these birthday gifts before he died. They would remain with me. I would wear the sweater with leggings during the last weeks of winter after the fire, and the sweater would stay in my closet.

The World Almanac became an addition to the bookshelf with the cover facing out, with the year he died in view.

Later, when my daughter was six, she would ask what it looks like inside the urn, and if I ever opened it. I'd tell her it probably looked gray like gray sand and I wasn't ready to open the urn yet and let his ashes fly away somewhere.

"When will you?" she asked.

I still don't know.

Sports Jacket

The funeral that didn't happen. If there hadn't been a fire, if his face had been identifiable and there wasn't a process to legally identify him by dental records and a fingerprint. If there had been a funeral with an open casket, I may have asked the funeral director to have my father wear the navy sports jacket.

I wonder if I held a funeral for my father what it would have been like. The problem with being estranged and not knowing his friends or family members, was the challenge of getting the word out. I think about his pocketknife, the conversation with the daughter of the foster family, the emails with his track buddy. Could I have contacted the local newspaper or his high school, would I have been resourceful and published an advisory asking those who knew him to come to his funeral? I still don't know. Then there was the expense of a funeral, but maybe I could have worked out a payment plan with the funeral home.

I might have asked that the sugar packets and tissues stay in the front pockets of the jacket for the service. If he had died another way, a gentler way, I might have still found his jacket in his car or in a closet at his home, but he had been cremated before I arrived at his car.

When I found the navy sports jacket in his car, hanging on the hook by the back door, with a plastic wrap around it, I knew it something he took care of and neatly set on the hanger for the next day. I imagine him alive wearing this jacket. One of last things he wore.

I bring the jacket close to me and inhale, it smells of cigarette smoke and has a muggy scent.

I notice on the emblem sewn on the inside, it's made by Learbury, right in the Syracuse area, the Italian family-run supplier of fine tailored clothing from back in the 1920s that has faded into history. Touching the collar, I see how it's sewn impeccably and looks hand-stitched, a jacket that keeps the back straight, and it means business with the two polished brass buttons at the front. It might have been the nicest thing he owned. I'm unsure where he got it from, maybe a thrift store.

While he went door to door handing out promotional flyers and curating leads for his sales job with the home improvement company, when he shook a hand I can imagine the three brass buttons at the cuff would shine and be noticed with the expectations of anything is possible.

The summer before he died, my father told me about the new place in the country in Phoenix, New York where the houses were spaced apart, the solitude, seclusion on a two-lane road.

There was another place, another house he talked about and was considering renting, but the landlord of the other home wanted more money for a deposit. I think about this other home and immediately what follows is at once a sense of roads, time and place, destiny. I know our choices can lead to darkness, turmoil, regret, unsaid goodbyes and death. This home. That home. I wonder if this home was the fate of my father's life, or if he could have had more years in the other home.

When I look at the jacket, I imagine my father getting ready for the day. I only have wonder; my memory goes far back to when his hair was fuller, at the green house, he is hacking and coughing and brushing his teeth. I do not know his morning routine as an older man, I do not know his mannerisms, but I imagine the sun not even up yet. His home might have creaked from the wind outside hitting the walls as my dad got into a rhythm shaving his face, the only sound the swish-swash splashing of the razor getting cleaned in the sink. His roommate would be sleeping, the home would be quiet as he hurried to finish up his morning routine.

He may have arched his eyebrow like James Dean at the mirror. He may have debated tweezing his gray wizard eyebrows, and then let his double-bridged eyeglasses fall down his nose, like an actor giving a strong stare to the camera, his eyes saying hell can't be worse than the ruts of yesterday.

Here the day is young, he remains frozen in time here, in the day before he died.

Where his forehead met his balding widow's peak, it creates a heart shape at his hairline. The vein on the side of his forehead relaxes before brushing his teeth, stained yellow from all the coffee, and it's a reminder about a dentist appointment he scheduled. (Only he wouldn't make the appointment. When all his calls were transferred to my phone, and when the receptionist called after he died to confirm the dentist appointment, I'd canceled it for him.)

As he combs his hair, maybe he reflects on the house he lived in with recovering alcoholics six months before. "I saved a life. I really did today," he said when he told me on the phone about a housemate at the halfway house he lived in before, who had left a paper plate near the burning flame on the stove. "These idiots don't know how to even turn off a stove. You see a flame; you turn it off. Turn the knob, fool. I'm living with a bunch of clowns."

He might have thought about when he had curly hair and let it go wild, nights of sharing his philosophies, telling stories, singing songs, waking up hung over after a night at the biker bar, Jumpin Jacks, where he was known as "the professor."

Then, over a light blue dress shirt, he may have worn a vest paired with navy wool pants, another thrift store find.

"I'm a frog in a suit," he had told me during one of our chats about making sales pitches door-to-door, with a flyer ready. Next, he'd put on his watch; I remember he had a habit of turning his hand to look under his wrist, where the face of his watch rested.

Outside the sun on snow would sparkle, and before stepping outside he may have checked his diabetes finger stick and used a glucometer. A couple years before he died, he was diagnosed with diabetes. I cannot be sure we had a detailed conversation about his medications or appointments. He may have said he gets his blood checked a couple times a week, maybe I had only been half listening on that call, but I didn't know much more until after he died, and I decided to gather his health records.

The records say he was complaining of polyuria and fatigue and started on metformin. The notes include that he was referred for a diabetic eye exam, he was made aware about foot care and dietary modifications. It says he checks his fingerstick one to two times a week. I read his A1c was 6.1, and there are other numbers I don't quite understand within the records, so I research online to learn more about his condition, and how he was managing his blood sugar levels.

Then I imagine a heavy brown winter jacket, brown boots, and a warm winter hat. After gathering his wallet, phone, and keys he'd walk out into the deep snow, to his car, to his sports jacket.

The stray cat with gray and black stripes that he mentioned was usually outside the door on warmer days is nowhere to be seen, as my father follows the footprints he'd left throughout the past week to his car. It would make sense for him to use a shovel more like a walking stick on some of the icy patches of snow. The sunlight on snow, the pathway made from steps taken yesterday, he might exhale a sigh into the chilly air, as though he made peace with his missteps and regrets. The sky is blue and there is more to do and more time, hours to fill, months, years to make up for lost time. He'd smoke a cigarette, which he may put out in the snow to save it for another time when he reaches the car.

Then everything goes gray.

I know he will die without warning before the next sunrise, and I will find the jacket, clipboard, thermos, pocketknife, and all that is left of his life will be found.

INTRODUCTIONS

My father's favorite candy was a Snickers and this treat has become a ritual I share with my kids. I love it when my daughter says, "Your dad would love this," while we chomp down the peanuts and chocolate. As my kids got older, I have shared with them my father's voice through his preserved voicemails and I share some keepsakes I have, I showed them their grandfather's Giant's hat and sports jacket. Showing these objects to my kids has been a way to have an answer when my kids ask about who their grandfather was.

A Memory Box

Inside a dresser drawer, or a desk, a big filing cabinet, stashed in a cardboard box in a garage or shed, up in an attic, are all places that artifacts of a life can be stored and found, but that wasn't the case. I had scrambled to put an obituary together for my father with what I did know about him, but I had been wrong about facts that summed up his life. It wasn't just because of the fire scorching his belongings, it was because the facts of his life were stories untold.

Overcome with shock and grief, processing that his life had ended, I rushed the writing process while constructing some final words about his life. My brain went blank, I couldn't think of one accolade or accomplishment to describe, I didn't have any documents to refer to, like a diploma or scrapbook with photos capturing the greatest moments of his life, and I didn't feel comfortable reaching out to his family who I hardly knew to write these final words about his life. I was without the resources to really understand the fullness of the years he had lived.

I will admit, one of the reasons I didn't have a big wedding was because I wasn't sure how to deal with his circumstances, I would have had to figure out where he would stay, what would he wear, if his car would make it down to Manhattan if he didn't want to fly, I would have to set up his flight, then a car service and hell, who would he sit next to at the reception.

Even though my marriage wouldn't last, I still think about how I didn't get to have that dance with him.

I felt embarrassed by his disheveled appearance and water-stained hat on those rare occasions I saw him in person and during his rants or during calls, when he had a phone. I hadn't asked enough questions about his childhood or teenage years, his ambitions, or proudest moments, I didn't expect him to say much about his childhood, I didn't care enough to ask, and I didn't expect him to die.

I figured there would be another time for those conversations, maybe when his life wasn't in shambles. But whether his life had been worthwhile or not, in the end, I was his next of kin, I had to find the words, I was the person who had known him best.

None of the above could be included in an obituary, so I wrote he was a great conversationalist and was extremely knowledgeable, a deep thinker. He could carry a tune. Instead of saying he had an alcohol addiction throughout his life, I wrote that he had been through his own struggles but had never lost his positive spirit. These were gentler words than the reality, I wrote that he believed in compassion as a common sense and referred to a voicemail, stating he recently had said, "Life is about fun if you don't hurt others, but then you have to at some point try to help others, and then your life is worth it."

I didn't include where he had attended high school or his time in the military, I wasn't sure. After the obituary was published in the Syracuse newspaper, I'd realize I had been wrong about his college path. A strange guilt and curiosity formed for not getting it right for him. I couldn't shake the thought that it was up to me to carry on who he was, and that the words I wrote were not enough.

Texas has been good for my grief. After moving here, away from my roots I felt an impulse to spend the time to uncover anything I could. It was the distance from New York, the longing that drew me closer to my father's history. I started prying, researching, emailing, calling, and mailing to gather documents of my father's life, and make my own memory box. It would later hold his health records, his diploma, a photo album specifically of photos of him, his yearbook, letters he wrote, and newspaper clippings about his death, voicemail transcribes I printed, I included in the box the phase of the moon before the early morning hours before he died, and so much more.

The heirlooms I found in his car started this searching, they brought the questions about the things I didn't know, and the questions led to finding the artifacts inside this box.

My favorite discovery is his health records. With my father's death certificate in hand, I requested my dad's records from the VA medical center in Syracuse, I had only expected a few pages of basic health stats, height, weight, maybe a medication he was taking, not one hundred pages that explained so many details about his life I didn't know about. The pages open into his emotional health and are a peek into the topics we never discussed about his alcohol addiction and mental health, but they are so much more. It's a gift, a big surprise to read these notes, that allows me and my father to connect now better than we ever have. Each page is a reminder that the history of our relatives can easily be forgotten or left in the dark if the stories are not sought and found. The paths we experienced during our lifetime are not promised to be remembered, or to be shared with younger generations, his grandchildren. The fullness of our lives can become simply short sentences, words explaining traits and a few highlights, maybe a passion or skill if we are lucky, these tid-bits of our life can be all that is left.

Now I have more words, the right words to explain my father's messy and complicated, eccentric, and imperfect life. I have a timeline of where, how and when.

Discovering more about what I didn't know has taken effort and patience, hours reading through these artifacts, and it has been emotionally exhausting at times to learn about his many issues he carried with him. Tears always are there, when I think about his brokenness, being without a car, without a phone, and sleeping at a homeless shelter, dark experiences I never got to discuss in detail were there in the shadows of our relationship, it makes my heart sore. I can make some peace with the pain in these words left unsaid because I get another chance to know him from these discoveries and because the memory box is nearly full.

FEBRUARY

My father's urn with his ashes inside is resting in the passenger seat. I wanted it to be one of the first things I placed in my new home. I would bring in next a couple suitcase of clothing and shoes, a box of plates, cups, forks and spoons, two chests with books, three blankets, a few pillows, my kid's favorite toys.

I lifted my father's urn, the wooden box with the mountainous landscape on the front faces my new home, the cheapest apartment I could find in my children's school district. The mortar between the bricks on the building is slapped together and splitting out, it doesn't have to be perfect. I keep telling myself this isn't forever. I look up to the second floor. There's a balcony and a big front window to let in some natural light. I balance my father's urn at the gate with one arm and opened it. There is no turning back.

Sweat forms quickly in the crease where I bend my arm and carry my father's urn up to the second floor. It's sweltering for February; the humid air holds a stickiness that I just can't get used to.

I crave the coziness of pulling through the arms of a sweater, the icy chill of snow, even slipping a little on ice. As a kid my father would knock down the thick icicles off the roof of my childhood home in February, the wind would seep through my scarf, I'd shiver but it would remind me the cold was a part of what was normal and the winter was long. Whenever I made a snow angel my inhales would hit the freezing air and create what felt like little icicles inside my nose. Snow banks were mountains to climb and my puffy snow pants would be slushy inside by the afternoon's end.

I wish I could ask him, *how did this happen, where am I, Dad*. He always hated the heat. *Well, here we are, still here in Texas.* I climbed the stairs to the second floor, then jiggle the key. *Almost there*, I say out loud.

A step forward means a division, a separation, a split, a divorce, I remember the mini wedding photo album, mailed to him. It must have burned in the fire.

I place my father's urn on the kitchen counter, but soon I will buy a bookshelf, his real spot.

I carry in a few books and a tote bag that holds my dad's keepsakes inside. In front of the bathroom mirror I place a new toothbrush holder and a soap pump. I pull at my marquise engagement ring. I add soap and pull again, it's warped. I get it off after a struggle. I didn't know when I was dreaming about the antique band and diamond bought in downtown Manhattan that it would pass through a decade to then be tucked away in drawer in Texas.

My kids, my only blood relatives here, I've seen every single day of their lives and now will see every other week. I do not know yet how much that will crush my heart because I cannot imagine a pain greater than finding out a parent has died in a fire, but the ache from missing my children will override this grief.

The new bunk beds have been a way for me to talk about the divorce with the kids, them going back and forth. This furniture, this February is life-changing.

I don't want to ache afterward from schlepping it in the apartment. I want it to land after being hauled somewhat quickly and signed for, without room to think about the weight of it on my back, so I clicked the option on the furniture store website offering free delivery and set up too, is worth the extra cost.

I told the sales lady I needed a bed for myself, a wood bed, something rustic and in my nervousness I said sarcastically, *just not a coffin*. Whatever is on sale. I sit on a mattress for a tenth of a second and say I will take it. Density and thickness, how deep I'll sink into it, isn't a concern of mine.

I decided on a red fabric couch, it can hold my children's pizza stains and spills, it's in my budget and can fit three people, and it comes with two complementary decorative pillows. The sales lady tried to convince me over a square table, it was a hundred dollars more than I wanted to spend. I told her I was thinking round, a glass center, brown faux leather chairs. I have already seen it on the store's website, it's the cheapest set.

These basics will liven up the plain walls, give this bare home some color, a pillow to lean back into, and a calm waves over me, there's comfort in knowing whenever my children enter our new home they will pass my father's urn.

GOODBYE FOR NOW

I had carried the grief for my father for a decade when the horrifying blaze of the Opera House of the Palais-Royal burning would catch me off guard while browsing the second floor of the Museum of Fine Arts in Houston.

I hadn't expected to be face-to-face with the 1781 fire and rising flames that engulfed the structure and gutted it. The oil painting by Hubert Robert, and its hellish haze in the sky, would hit the core of me.

The front of the opera house with the windows hollowed out would remind me of my father's home, the disturbing vision surfaced from my heart. The unexpected fall of ice hitting the gas line, the rapid ignition from the heater. My father sound sleep. Seconds left before the explosion. Perhaps just allowing a single gasp before he attempted to dart down the hallway, where he had been found by firemen.

I stare hard at the painting and the smokey air above the opera house. I imagined the sound of sirens down the country road and the snow full of charred debris and smut, the smell of burnt metal and scorched wood consuming the air. I still need a moment to regroup my mind after all this time, because the emotional baggage, the trauma of sudden loss doesn't just go away with time. Grieving after a sudden loss can be complex and traumatic, and when a death happens without warning, without a goodbye, the shock and coping mechanisms can take a long time to navigate, as the sorrow simply seems to stick around. Robert's painting of the opera house aflame is a unique artifact from a heartbreaking day. The amber and smokey air spoke to my silence and sadness, I process what has been lost and the years in between my dad here and gone. It might sound supernatural, but I imagine his energy rising above it, already with me miraculously when the sheriff called, as though his spirit was somehow in the doorway of that conversation. I hold onto this thought, there is acceptance and peace within the thought, it allows me to walk into the new day as the years go by and I accept that bereaved is just who I will always be.

Later, I'd read online about the opera fire, how while the destructive fire raged through the building the cries of theater goers awoke the district. I stare at the bottom of the painting, where figures of people, perhaps running away, are seen.

While other museum visitors eased their way through the gallery that day passing the dark and red colors, the blasted windows, the doomed dark paint, I remained there. The loss propelled from the painting somehow connected to the unsaid goodbyes and lost time that still crushes me. I wipe my eyes and purposely give the ashy colors my time.

"You have to at some point try to help others. And then your life is worth it."

—a voicemail from Isobella Jade's father

The author would like to thank earlier readers and editors, and especially Daniel Stern, Kathy Schneider and Edward Ash-Milby. Thank you to my family for their support, and especially my mother for all the chats about writing and books.

Isobella Jade is an author and essayist, her deeply personal and lyrical essays about parenting, grief, longing and nature have appeared in The New York Times, SheKnows, Houston Chronicle, Glamour, Insider, and others. Originally from New York, she currently lives in Houston.